NIPPON POP

Steve McClure

Tuttle Publishing
Tokyo • Singapore • Boston

For Rie

Published by Charles E. Tuttle Publishing,
an imprint of Periplus Editions (HK) Ltd.

© 1998 by Steve McClure
All rights reserved

LCC Card No. 97-60297
ISBN 0-8048-2107-0
JASRAC #9801561-801

First Edition, 1998

Editorial Offices:
Japan
Charles E. Tuttle Publishing Co., Inc.
2-6, Suido 1-chome,
Bunkyo-ku, Tokyo 112-0005, Japan

Singapore
Periplus (Singapore) Pte Ltd
5 Little Road #08-01
Singapore 536983, Singapore

Distributors
USA
Charles E. Tuttle Company, Inc.
Airport Industrial Park
RR1 Box 231-5
North Clarendon, VT 05759, USA
Tel: (802) 773-8930
Fax: (802) 773-6993

Japan
Tuttle Shokai, Inc.
1-21-13 Seki
Tama-ku, Kawasaki-shi
Kanagawa-ken 214-0022, Japan
Tel: (81) (44) 833-0225
Fax: (81) (44) 822-0413

Southeast Asia
Berkeley Books Pte Ltd.
5 Little Road #08-01
Singapore 536983, Singapore
Tel: (65) 280-3320
Fax: (65) 280-6290

Creative Director
Christina Ong

Designers
Chie Arakawa
William Atyeo
Matt Percival
Rupert Singleton
Christopher Wadsworth

Editorial
Erica Keirstead
Brenton Wong

Translations by Kay Irie

Printed in Singapore

Contents

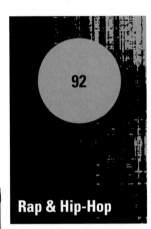
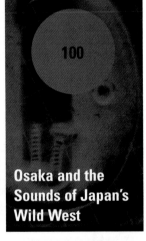

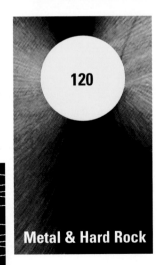

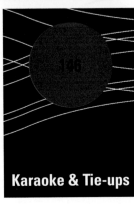
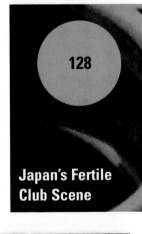

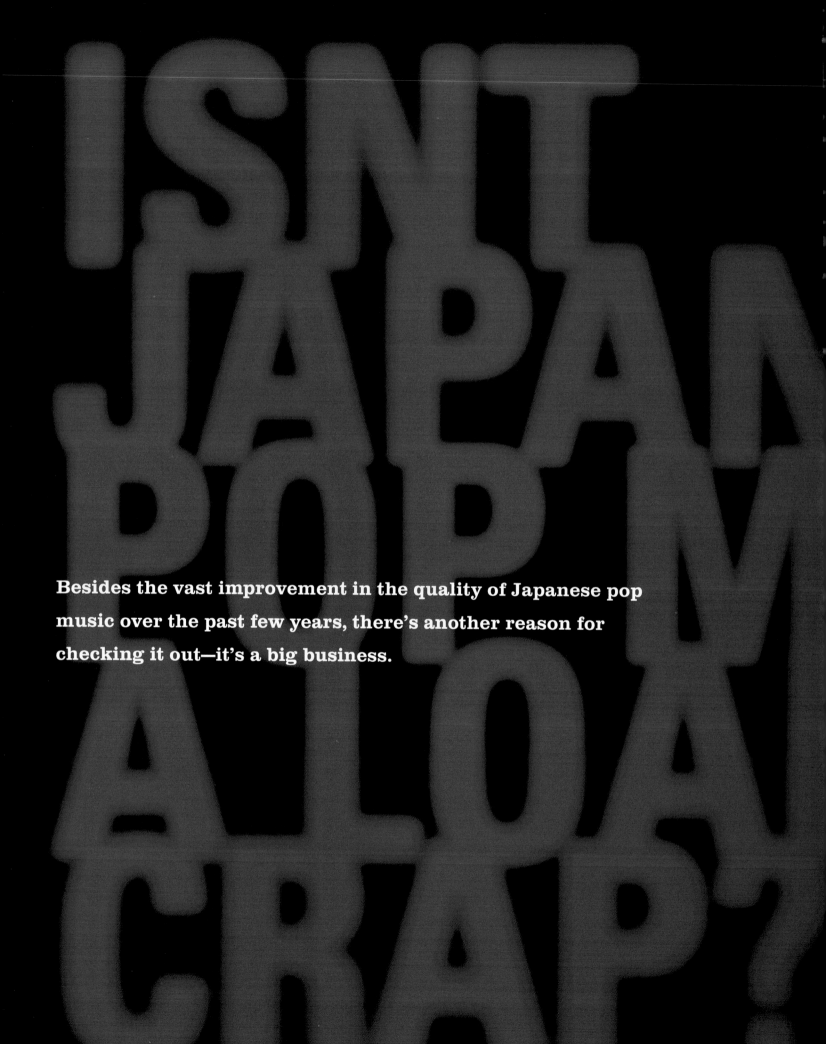

ISNT JAPAN POP MUSIC A LOAD A CRAP?

Besides the vast improvement in the quality of Japanese pop music over the past few years, there's another reason for checking it out—it's a big business.

Japanese pop music? Nothing but a bunch of cute-but-can't-sing idols with shelf lives only slightly longer than tofu, right?

Wrong. Some of the most interesting, challenging, and just plain good music being made on the planet today comes from Japan.

While innovative acts like Pizzicato Five, Super Junky Monkey, and the Pugs have opened the eyes of some people overseas to the wacky world of Japanese pop, it's still tough to find quality stuff amid all the bland mainstream pop that dominates the music scene.

In this book, I've tried to focus on the truly original music now being made in Japan, while also providing an overview of the industry as a whole, and background information where relevant. With its emphasis on the current scene, Nippon Pop is not intended to be a history of Japanese pop music, but rather a highly subjective look at an aspect of pop culture that changes from day to day. My own biases and interests inevitably color the book. No doubt I've left out many people's favorite artists, for which I can only offer my humble and groveling apologies.

Besides the vast improvement in the quality of Japanese pop music over the past few years, there's another reason for checking it out—it's a big business. Virtually everyone on the planet knows how great Japan's electronics industry is (do you know anyone who doesn't own a Sony Walkman?), but it's shocking how little the average Westerner knows about this multibillion dollar industry. If you're a serious student of pop music, you can hardly afford to overlook Japan.

Let's get one thing straight, though: Japan's take on rock 'n' roll, pop—call it what you will—is just as valid as anybody else's. Thirty years ago, rock was still seen as an exotic foreign import in Japan. But now it's just as natural for a Tokyo teenager to pick up a guitar and rail against society as it is for a kid in Milwaukee or Manchester.

So cast off your preconceptions and get ready for a musical journey that will take you into some of the most exotic and fascinating sonic territory imaginable.
—Steve McClure
Tokyo, 1998

Acknowledgments

With grateful thanks to the following people for their help and support:

Kaoru Kitamoto, Keiko Oya, Shiori Inoue, Katsumi Nishimura, Kaz Fukatsu, Keith Cahoon, Hitomi Suzuki, Phil Gayle, Masa Matsuzaki, Mamoru Murakami, Tom Yoda, Yukinao Tanaya, Kumiko Sakurai, Kyoko Sakuma, Hiroshi Otomo, Carol Abe, Peter Barakan, Peter Buckleigh, David Friedman, Keith McPhalen, Erica Keirstead, Chie Arakawa, Adam White, Thom Duffy, Terri MacMillan, Mike Rogers, Ken Watanabe, Mitsuaki Iwase, Makoto Taniguchi, Jonny Thompson, Lisa Kyoko Isobe, Hoppy Kamiyama, Keiko Yajima, Bryan Harrell, Takako Saeki, Mark Schumacher, Gilles Kennedy, Mariko Kurokawa, Alex Abramoff, Reiko Meguro, Masako Nakaya, Maureen Donald, and my parents.

In memory of Miki Fujita.

KUTS

音

ROOTS

Roots of
J
APANESE POP

松田聖子や美空ひばりよりも昔、録音技術が普及する遥か以前からポップ・ミュージック（大衆音楽）は常に日本に存在していた。盆踊りなどで演奏されてきた民謡や大阪の河内音頭などである。それは田や畑で働いている間に歌われたり、地元の祭事で歌われたりした純粋な意味でのポップ・ミュージックであったと言えよう。明治維新後、ブラスバンド、浪曲、浅草オペラ、宝塚歌劇、広い意味でのジャズ、ハワイアンなどさまざまな形で洋楽の影響を受けたポップ・ミュージックが広まったが、敗戦後進駐軍がもたらしたFENラジオの果たした役割は大きく、50年代に入ると日本人によるロカビリーバンドが結成され、ミッキー・カーチスらのスターが生まれた。現在日本のポップ・ミュージックの中心は歌謡曲と呼ばれるジャンル。歌謡曲の定義はかなり曖昧ではあるが、大衆路線ということで理解できる。中でも故古賀政男は最高の作曲家とされている。

BEFORE SEIKO MATSUDA,

before Hibari Misora, before recording technology was even invented, there was Japanese pop music. It was pop music in the purest sense—music by, for and of the people, the kind of music that ordinary Japanese sang to pass the time while working in the fields or whooping it up at local festivals.

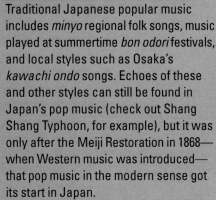

Traditional Japanese popular music includes *minyo* regional folk songs, music played at summertime *bon odori* festivals, and local styles such as Osaka's *kawachi ondo* songs. Echoes of these and other styles can still be found in Japan's pop music (check out Shang Shang Typhoon, for example), but it was only after the Meiji Restoration in 1868—when Western music was introduced—that pop music in the modern sense got its start in Japan.

Between 1868 and 1945, Japanese pop encompassed military and brass band music (which you can still hear on the streets of Japan courtesy of the right-wing *uyoku* sound trucks), Osaka's *rokyoku* (also known as *naniwabushi*) narrative songs, chanson, the show music of the Takarazuka all-girl revue (an acquired taste, to be sure), jazz (in the broad, prewar sense of the term, encompassing dance music and straight pop songs), tango, and Hawaiian music.

The 1945–52 Occupation of Japan by the victorious Allied Forces resulted in a huge influx of American popular culture, including music. The U.S. Armed Forces' Far East Network (FEN) radio service played a crucial role in this regard. Many Japanese musicians and music fans got their first taste of genres such as country music, rockabilly, and modern jazz, thanks to FEN.

In the mid-'50s many Japanese musicians formed country-western or rockabilly bands. One star from that era, multiracial singer Mickey Curtis, who made his debut with the C&W band Crazy West in 1958, is still active today.

The main pop music style was *kayokyoku*, a loosely defined term that one authoritative guide to Japanese pop music describes as "Japanese MOR (middle of the road) music." The late Masao Koga is considered to have been the greatest kayokyoku songwriter.

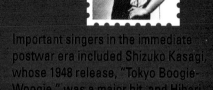

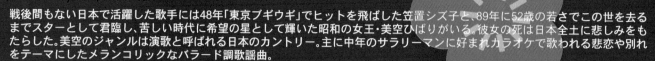

Important singers in the immediate postwar era included Shizuko Kasagi, whose 1948 release, "Tokyo Boogie-Woogie," was a major hit, and Hibari

戦後間もない日本で活躍した歌手には48年「東京ブギウギ」でヒットを飛ばした笠置シズ子と、89年に52歳の若さでこの世を去るまでスターとして君臨し、苦しい時代に希望の星として輝いた昭和の女王・美空ひばりがいる。彼女の死は日本全土に悲しみをもたらした。美空のジャンルは演歌と呼ばれる日本のカントリー。主に中年のサラリーマンに好まれカラオケで歌われる悲恋や別れをテーマにしたメランコリックなバラード調歌謡曲。

Misora, who remained a major star until her untimely death at age 52 in 1989, which sent the entire nation into mourning. Misora's forte was *enka*, a type of melancholy kayokyoku ballad that usually deals with themes such as doomed love affairs and painful separations.

Traditionally based on the Japanese minor pentatonic scale, enka occupies a place in Japanese pop music similar to that of country music in the United States. Call it cryin'-in-your-sake music. Enka's biggest fans are middle-aged salarymen, who croon along to their favorite tunes in Japan's myriad karaoke bars.

A singer and an actress, Misora was known as the "Queen of Japanese singers" and the "Queen of the Showa era." ("Showa" is the era name given to the 1926-1989 reign of the emperor known in the West as Hirohito.) The daughter of a Yokohama fish monger, she made her professional debut in 1949, becoming a symbol of hope for the Japanese during the desperate economic conditions after the war.

Misora was the first Japanese pop music star to cause fans to go absolutely nuts. In 1956 ten people were either killed or injured when an audience waiting to get into one of her concerts rushed the hall. In the following year, a 19-year-old girl threw hydrochloric acid on Misora's face, resulting in minor injuries to the star.

In the six months following Misora's death in June 1989, sales of her recordings increased no less than twenty-five times over the first half of that year. There was even a concert in which an orchestra provided live instrumental backing for Misora's recorded voice, while a single spotlight illuminated an empty stage – kind of a karaoke seance. Misora remains a popular subject for Japan's mass-circulation weeklies.

Hibari Misora
美空ひばり

Kayokyoku Tradition

歌謡曲史を駆け足で振り返るなら東京のカフカフドゴシコのライブを見るのも悪くない。蒸し暑い東京の夜、渋谷駅前でカフカフの3人が会社帰りの人の流れの中、ストリートライブを行っている。シンガー荒谷葉子に注目が集まる。浴衣に身を包みレトロ調で60年代の銀座の様子を歌う「東京ウキウキ」。レゲエのリズムとキーボードやギター、テープオケがファンキーで新しい感覚だがそれは紛れもなく歌謡曲の伝統を受け継ぐ。

歌謡曲

For a quick course in kayokyoku, you could do worse than check out a live show by Tokyo band Kafu Kafu Dogo Shiko.

On a recent hot, sultry Tokyo evening, three members of KKDS are performing a "street live" for the crowds of commuters passing through Tokyo's Shibuya Station. Singer Yohco Aratani is the focus of attention. Her colorful summer kimono, old-fashioned hairdo, and stylized moves add to the retro appeal of the song, "Tokyo Uki Uki." It describes Ginza in the early '60s before it lost out to such areas as Roppongi and Shibuya as the center of Tokyo nightlife. But the reggae beat laid down by her accompanying keyboardist and guitarist (augmented by backing tapes) gives the tune an updated, funky appeal that makes the music hard to categorize.

Central to the band's identity is their identification with the rich heritage of kayokyoku.

"After the war, there was a great kayokyoku composer in Japan called Ryoichi Hattori," explains band leader Masaharu Kamura. "He mixed various kinds of music, like jazz from the U.S. and enka from Korea, into his songs. We're like that, but in our case we mix in reggae, rock, jazz— anything."

"We grew up with foreign music," adds Aratani. "But we still have a Japanese mindset. We want to express the sounds of a new generation of Japanese."

No matter how many ingredients KKDS tosses into its musical brew, the essence of kayokyoku—a catchy, lighthearted melody with a definite "Oriental" feel—is always there. A good example is the opening track on their mini-album, *Matsuri no Yoru ni*, which features an extremely busy, funky instrumental track over which Aratani's vocals soar majestically.

Besides kayokyoku, elements of reggae, samba, jazz, funk, and rock can be found in KKDS's music. "Each one of us has their own musical taste, and that makes it hard to categorize our style of music," says Kamura. "In fact, a lot of record companies told us that our music couldn't fit into any genre."

Instead of concentrating all their energies on getting a TV drama or commercial "tie-up" for one of their songs, KKDS have emphasized taking their music to the people by continuing "street live" dates like the one in Shibuya, playing at elementary schools, and traveling to Beijing for a special concert put on by a Japan-China cultural association.

The band's name has puzzled more than a few people. Kamura says it's onomatopoeic. "When I was imitating the sound of samba music to explain it to the younger members, I went, 'kafu, kafu, dogo shico,'" he explains.

"We grew up with foreign music," adds Aratani. "But we still have a Japanese mindset. We want to express the sounds of a new generation of Japanese."

"Sukiyaki," Eleki Bands, and Group Sounds

The only Japanese artist to have any appreciable impact in the West (until Pink Lady's unlikely stab at the American market in the '70s) was the late Kyu Sakamoto, whose rendition of "Ue o Muite Aruko" (known overseas as "Sukiyaki") went all the way to No. 1 on the Billboard singles chart in 1963—a feat no other Japanese artist has ever achieved.

Inspired by the guitar-based instrumental music of the Ventures (who ever since the early '60s have toured Japan every year, causing some uncharitable types to label them the "Dentures"), many Japanese musicians took up the electric guitar in the mid-'60s in the eleki bands era, which is recalled in the film "Seishun Den Deke Deke Deke" ("seishun" means youth, "den deke deke deke" is onomatopoeic for the sound of Ventures-style electric guitar).

The next phase was the "group sounds" boom of the 1960s, in which Japanese musicians, inspired by groups like the Beatles and the Rolling Stones, formed bands where the electric guitar was again the main instrument but in which vocals were also emphasized. They included the Tigers, the Spiders, the Beavers, the Peacocks, the Fingers, the Jet Brothers, and the Jaguars.

Those names sound silly today, but back in the '60s, Western rock was considered a corrupting foreign influence on the "pure" youth of Japan. Right-wing nationalists mounted large-scale protests when the Beatles performed at Tokyo's Budokan in 1966—but they couldn't prevent rock from becoming part of the Japanese cultural mainstream.

the 70s

In the '70s, Japanese rock began to find its own voice. Pioneering Japanese rock groups of the 1970s included Flower Traveling Band; Carmen Maki and Oz; the Sadistic Mika Band; Happy End, whose alumni include Yellow Magic Orchestra co-founder Haruomi Hosono; Zuno Keisatsu (Brain Police); Sugar Babe, from which emerged solo artists Taeko Onuki and Tatsuro Yamashita (the latter is one of the true geniuses of Japanese pop); and RC Succession. This last band produced solo stars Kiyoshiro Imawano and Reichi Nakaido, whose rare live shows are unrivaled for their intensity.

The 1970s also saw the "new music" boom, in which singer/songwriters such as Miyuki Nakajima and Yumi Matsutoya Yumi (aka "Yuming") gained popularity for their sophisticated, personal approach.

In the late '70s three things happened that had a major influence on Japanese pop. The first was the "idol boom," in which performers such as Seiko Matsuda, Momoe Yamaguchi, Hiromi Go, and Hideki Saijo captured the hearts and wallets of millions of teenagers nationwide.

The second was Yellow Magic Orchestra, a three-man group (Haruomi Hosono, Ryuichi Sakamoto, and Yukihiro Takahashi) whose brilliant synthesizer-based style of pop music has had an enormous influence on musicians all over the world (see Electronic, Techno, and Ambient).

The third big development in Japanese pop in this era was the debut of Shoukichi Kina and his band Champloose, which first brought the music of Okinawa, Japan's southernmost prefecture, to the attention of mainstream pop fans (see Ethnic Pop).

70年代は日本のポップ・ミュージックに大きな影響を与えた。はっぴいえんどやRCサクセション等日本オリジナルのロックが誕生。この中から後に活躍するソロアーティストが数多く生まれる。また、同時期に中島みゆきやユーミンによるニューミュージックブームも起こり、70年代後半には山口百恵や西城秀樹らのアイドルブーム、YMOのテクノ、喜納昌吉&チャンプルーズによる沖縄音楽のポップ化と今のJポップを形作る重要な動きがあった。

THE BAND BOOM

In the late '80s the late-night TV program "Ikaten" featured amateur and semi-pro bands, giving rise to the "band boom." Suddenly, honest-to-God rock 'n' roll was back on the Japanese musical agenda, and that scared a lot of people in the industry who were more accustomed to dealing with pre-packaged "talent." But the boom ended almost as quickly as it began, as the mass media shifted its attention to the next "boom": dance music and the "Juliana's" phenomenon.

"During the band boom, the fans treated bands like some kind of fashion; they were only interested in how they looked," noted Miki Ohno, who played guitar and sang with Passengers, one of the better groups to come out of the band boom, in one interview. "On top of that, because so many bands had been formed by so many bad musicians, the musicians lacked any kind of musical integrity and just created music that would make money.

"I think most Japanese music fans are deaf," added a clearly bitter Ohno. "In Japan, no one has any critical awareness; they just follow the media and each other."

But it can't be denied that since then there's been a steady evolution in Japanese rock and pop away from slavish imitation of foreign models toward music that's more confident, professional, and self-assured.

The '80s also saw the "live house" club scene produce great no-nonsense rock bands like the Blue Hearts and the Street Sliders, while the Sunday *hokoten* scene in Tokyo's Yoyogi Park spawned major talents such as The Boom.

With the beginning of the '90s the Japanese music scene shifted into yet another phase as million-selling hits became the norm, thanks in large part to the "tie-up" phenomenon. At the same time, the public's taste in music became more fragmented and sophisticated as the indies scene blossomed and foreign music stores Tower, Virgin, and HMV shook up the market. By the middle of the decade, some of the most interesting, incredible, and sometimes just plain insane music on the planet was coming out of Japan—a fact that some people outside of Japan were beginning to appreciate.

80年代後半「イカ天」バンドブームで突然の「本物」のロック人気に、パッケージ化された音楽に馴れ切っていた業界は慌てる。が、その関心もすぐさま次のダンスブームへと移行。又、この時代ライブハウスや代々木のホコ天も注目を浴び、ザ・ブームやブルーハーツ等が才能を開花させた。90年代にはタイアップ／メガヒット時代が到来、と同時に市場も細分化が進みインディーズも活発化、Jポップは海外からの注目を浴び出している。

One of the Japanese pop music world's most important annual rituals is "Kohaku Uta Gassen" ("Red and White Song Contest"), which is broadcast on semi-public NHK TV on New Year's Eve. The format has been the same since the first Kohaku (on radio), back in 1951: Japan's top singers are divided into male and female teams, and a panel of judges decides which team has won—not that anybody really cares.

KOHAKU

紅白

The whole point of Kohaku is to include the latest hitmakers as well as veteran enka and kayokyoku singers and so reinforce the (sometimes pleasant, sometimes smothering) illusion that Japan is after all one big happy family. Many young Japanese consider the program hopelessly square, and acts like Mr. Children and Southern All Stars make a point of not appearing on Kohaku. But the program is a must-see for anyone seriously interested in Japanese pop— just be sure you have a big bottle of sake close at hand.

Jポップにおいて年に一度の大切なイベントは、大晦日にNHKで放送される紅白歌合戦。51年のラジオでの放送開始以来、番組形式は変わっていない。男女に分かれたトップシンガーが歌を競い審査員が勝敗を決める（誰も勝負にこだわってはいないが）。大切なのは旬のアーティストとベテラン演歌歌手らが一緒に歌い、日本は平和で皆仲良く暮らしているという幻想に浸ること。Jポップに興味があるならば必見の番組であることは間違いない。

外国人が日本のポップ・ミュージックをくだらないと軽蔑する理由は、そのアイドルの目覚ましい活躍にある。何人ものアイドルのバックミュージシャンを務めた東京のトップアンダーグラウンド・アーティストいわく、「彼(女)達はアーティストではなく歌手であり、時にはその歌すら満足に歌えない」。アイドル現象は個性を犠牲にし、従順を好み、和を重んじる日本の社会を反映している。アイドルのプロモーター達はレコードを出すだけではなく、彼／彼女達を様々な分野でオールラウンドに活躍できるタレントに仕立て上げ、比較的短いタレント生命を、人気が続く限り最大限に活かそうとする。(幸いにも)アイドルがトップチャートを独占する時代は過ぎ去った。とはいえ、ルックス先行のポップスターはまだまだ健在である。

The Ido

Japan's very visible "idol" pop stars are one big reason many foreigners dismiss Japanese pop music as a load of crap.

Notes a leading Tokyo underground-music figure, who has worked as a backing musician for several idol acts, "They're not artists—they're just singers—and sometimes they can't even sing."

One explanation for the idol phenomenon is that they reflect the values of a society that puts a premium on conformity (mediocrity, to be less charitable) at the expense of individuality. Non-threatening, non-controversial role models are useful tools in maintaining social harmony. Idols usually do a lot more than just make records. Their backers try to maximize their investment by positioning them as all-around entertainers and media personalities—*tarento*—with a high public profile during their relatively brief careers. Although the days when idols almost totally dominated the Japanese hit charts are (thankfully) long gone, there are still a lot of long-on-looks, short-on-talent popsters out there.

Seiko Matsuda

松田聖子ほどアイドルぶりを体現した歌手もいない。(予想に反した)長いレコーディングキャリアと数々のスキャンダルは彼女をポップ界の頂点へと引き上げた。福岡出身、78年16才でデビュー。高校卒業と同時の80年に初レコード「青い珊瑚礁」をリリース。80年代の典型的アイドルそのものだった松田は決して魅惑的ではないが、隣の妹的可愛さと上目使いの表情で人気を得る。そして80年3枚目のレコード「風は秋色」を皮切りにその後8年間で24枚連続1位獲得という偉業を成し遂げた。90年代が始まると純情

More than anyone else, Seiko Matsuda personifies the idol concept. Her (perhaps unexpectedly) long recording career and various personal scandals have elevated her to the highest level of the pop pantheon—now she is simply famous for being famous.

Matsuda, who grew up in Fukuoka, on the island of Kyushu, was discovered in 1978 at age 16 when she entered a "Miss 17" talent contest sponsored by Sony. "They said, 'Just send your picture and tape, and you can be a star,'" she says. "I just sent them, and it happened."

Her recording career began in 1980 with the single "Aoi Sangosho" following her graduation from high school. Her '80s publicity photos are typical of that era—she has a clued-out expression, slightly crossed eyes, and a cute-but-not-glamorous look. Back then, the template for Japanese idols was very much the girl (or boy) next door look—

non-threatening, reassuring, safe.

Matsuda's third single, "Kaze wa Akiiro," was the first of twenty-four consecutive Japanese No. 1 singles between 1980 and 1988. Her best-selling albums were 1983's *Utopia* and *Canary*, each of which sold 900,000 units (this was in the days before Tetsuya Komuro, Chage and Aska, and Dreams Come True made multimillion sellers the norm).

As the '90s began, Matsuda's demure, innocent image began to change, both off-stage and on. Her personal life attracted the scrutiny of Japanese scandal sheets, while the video of her 1995 single "It's Style" featured a sexily attired Seiko wrapping herself around a pole (that's a lowercase "p," by the way). She began to affect a much more glamorous look, and rumors of cosmetic surgery began to make the rounds.

In 1990 she tried her luck in the American market, releasing an English-language album on Columbia Records (part of CBS, which Sony had just bought) titled *Seiko*. The dance-oriented album included the single "The Right Combination," a duet with Donnie Wahlberg of New Kids On The Block. The album didn't chart, although the single made it into the lower reaches of Billboard's dance chart.

"Sony spent a lot of money on that release in the States in 1990, but nothing really came out of it," one Japanese source says.

"Sony Japan bought (the) American company, so they would send Japanese

artists to America to do something," Matsuda told Billboard when preparing for her second stab at the U.S. market in 1996. "My feeling was, 'OK, I'll do this,' but it was not strong."

In the mid-'90s, Matsuda still wanted to crack the tough American market. Sony was apparently less enthusiastic.

The company, say industry insiders, was reluctant to again try to break her internationally after the *Seiko* debacle.

In late 1995 Matsuda shocked the Japanese music biz by leaving Sony and signing a deal with Mercury Music Entertainment, part of the PolyGram group. The shift came when her popularity was on the wane. Her last Sony album, *It's Style '95*, sold just 260,000 units.

Unfortunately, her second English-language album, *Was It the Future*, recorded in L.A. with American musicians, also failed to chart in the U.S., despite being a pretty convincing, slickly produced slice of pop-soul. In contrast, the Japanese-language album she recorded at the same time in L.A. (with Japanese musicians) sold reasonably well back in Japan.

Despite—or because of—such ups and downs, Matsuda is still one of Japan's highest-profile celebrities. When a magazine or newspaper writes a banner headline with the name "Seiko"—a common-enough Japanese name—there's no doubt to whom it refers. In a country where women are supposed to stay in the background, she is a role model for assertive women.

SEIKO

なイメージは公私ともに変化を見せ始め、スキャンダルにも事欠かなくなる。95年リリースのビデオ『It's Style』ではセクシーさを強調。整形の噂も絶えない。90年、95年とアメリカ進出を試みるものの失敗。このような浮き沈みにも関わらず（もしくはそのお陰で？）、国内では今だにトップの地位にあり、数少ない強い女の象徴となっている。

70年代アイドルブームの申し子ピンクレディ。高校同級生ミーとケイは完璧な歌と踊りのコンビネーションでトップを極める。日本人スターとして唯一米国でもTV番組を持った程の人気だった。しかし日本独特のアイドルの輸出は文化的に無理があったようだ。一方、国内では「渚のシンドバット」「ウォンテッド」「UFO」など次々とミリオンセラーを出した。81年に解散するも96年に再結成。元祖ダンスアイドルとしてステージに立った。

Pink Lady

Typical of the '70s idol boom was the two-girl act Pink Lady. Mie (Mitsuyo Nemoto) and Kei (Keiko Masuda), high school friends from the city of Shizuoka, perfected a singing and dancing act that propelled them to the very top of the Japanese showbiz pantheon. They even had a TV show in the U.S.—the first and only Japanese pop act ever to do so. It was a less than overwhelming success, however. The term "culture-specific" comes to mind when talking about attempts to transplant Japanese idol acts into other markets.

Back in Japan, though, Pink Lady racked up a series of million-selling singles: "Nagisa No Shindobaddo," "Wanted," and "UFO." They broke up in 1981, but in late 1996 they decided to get back together to show the new generation of idols how it's really done.

Sixteen-year-old entertainer Kyoko Date is a manager's dream come true. "She doesn't complain about anything, and she doesn't get sick," says Kaz Hori, vice president of HoriPro Inc., Date's management agency. And she doesn't demand the kind of inflated salaries that many Japanese idols get. Date (pronounced "dah-tay"), who lives with her parents in a typical Tokyo suburb, debuted as a TV commercial "image girl" in 1996, and then released her first album. HoriPro also landed her parts in movies and TV dramas, and a CD-ROM featuring her is in the works.

If she sounds too good to be true, well, she is. Date is the world's first "virtual idol." She only exists as a computer-graphic image.

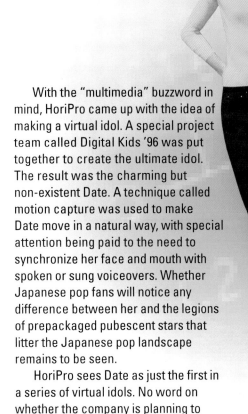

With the "multimedia" buzzword in mind, HoriPro came up with the idea of making a virtual idol. A special project team called Digital Kids '96 was put together to create the ultimate idol. The result was the charming but non-existent Date. A technique called motion capture was used to make Date move in a natural way, with special attention being paid to the need to synchronize her face and mouth with spoken or sung voiceovers. Whether Japanese pop fans will notice any difference between her and the legions of prepackaged pubescent stars that litter the Japanese pop landscape remains to be seen.

HoriPro sees Date as just the first in a series of virtual idols. No word on whether the company is planning to develop a virtual manager.

Kyoko Date

どんなに忙しくても一言も文句を言わないそんな理想的なタレント、伊達杏子は世界初のバーチャルアイドル。ホリプロがマルチメディア時代に向けてデジタルキッズ'96なるプロジェクトチームを結成し、モーション・キャプチャーをはじめとする技術を駆使、究極のアイドルを作り上げた。96年には既にファーストアルバムをリリース、TVCM、映画、TVドラマ、CD-ROMにも出演している。バーチャルアイドルの時代はやってくるのか?!

Discovering

A loudly dressed young man with greasy hair stops a demure high school girl on a busy Tokyo street. At first she feigns indifference, but then stops to listen.

"A pretty girl like you can be a star!" is his not-terribly-original pitch. He could be just a tout for Japan's huge sex industry, which explains his target's initial hesitation to stop and listen to his spiel. Or he could be a talent scout for one of Japan's powerful production companies, which are always looking for new faces to be the models, TV personalities, movie stars, and pop music idols of tomorrow.

She decides to listen, knowing that some of Japan's top entertainers have been discovered in just this way, although if she's not careful, her entertainment career could consist mainly of horizontal roles in adult films. On the other hand, fame and fortune—well, fame, at least—could be just around the corner.

Although the role of production companies, especially old-line firms, is starting to weaken, they're still a powerful force in Japanese showbiz. Their influence stems from their ability to take kids off the street and turn them into pre-packaged idols ready for public consumption, as well as from the absence in Japan of powerful independent managers and entertainment lawyers.

Record companies traditionally have left it to the agencies to come up with bankable stars, since they're not prepared to take the risk of signing talent without going through an agency.

Agencies can sign potential artists when they are as young as 12 or 13, with parents or guardians signing what can be extremely exploitative contracts on their behalf. The slightest hint of scandal on the artist's part—homosexuality or illegal drug use, for example—is grounds for cancellation by the agency. Ten-year contracts aren't uncommon.

The future star is then carefully groomed and educated under the company's supervision before making his or her debut. When the time is ripe, the production company makes a master recording and starts talking to record labels.

Once a deal is signed, the artist may still receive a salary instead of royalties based on their record sales (if they do receive royalties, they can be as low as 0.5%).

Successful artists often resent being paid a salary that may not have increased all that much since the days when they were unknowns being readied for the big time. As for the agencies, they feel entitled to the lion's share of the royalties, given their investment in the artist in the years before they made it big.

The artist may succeed in getting more money out of the agency. If not, he or she may buy out their contract and go off and start their own production agency. Many of Japan's top production firms, in fact, are run by former artists.

Many artists, however, simply enjoy their fame, untroubled by thoughts of the future, until like a superannuated baseball player or a clapped-out racehorse, they're dropped.

Sometimes memories are the only legacy of an idol's showbiz career.

"I was one of the most famous singers in Japan, and I have nothing to show for it," says a Tokyo housewife (who wishes to remain anonymous) who in the late '70s was one of Japan's top idols.

Older production agencies place a great deal of emphasis on getting their stars on TV, which means that appearance is at least as important as actual musical talent.

In contrast, the music itself is the priority for agencies such as Amuse, Being, and Burning which started coming onto the scene from the early '80s. Their rosters contain a higher proportion of bands as opposed to solo artists.

Although the rather depressing scenario outlined above still happens, things are changing.

"Many artists are now waking up," says Shoo Kusano, president of Shinko Music Publishing Co., which also manages artists such as Super Junky Monkey and Princess Princess, until the latter band's 1996 breakup. "They are already receiving direct copyright royalties from JASRAC (the Japanese Society for Rights of Authors, Composers and Publishers) ."

The traditional "slave" contract is becoming a thing of the past. Young Japanese are now much more worldly wise than previous generations.

Despite the horror stories, production agencies are constantly besieged by youngsters who want to see their name—or the name the production agency gives them—in lights.

Idols

" A pretty girl like you can be a star! "

Johnny's Jimusho

少年隊、光ゲンジ、SMAPなど新しい才能を発掘し世に送り出すことにかけてジャニーズ事務所社長・ジャニー北川にはかなわない。彼が探し出してくるタレントの多くは笑顔の魅力的なハンサムな少年達だが、パターンが決まっているわけではないと言う。テレビ出演やコンサート活動に重きがおかれ、レコードは二の次。80年代にローラースケートとそのルックスで一世を風靡した光ゲンジの初レコード・リリースは、以外にもデビュー7年後だった。

"I get three hundred letters a day from all over Japan from guys wanting to be members of Johnny's," says Johnny Kitagawa, president of production agency Johnny & Associates, aka Johnny's Jimusho.

TOKIO

Kitagawa's agency has an unsurpassed track record when it comes to finding new talent and marketing it to the Japanese public. Over the years, Johnny's has introduced a steady stream of top-selling groups, such as Shonentai, Hikaru Genji, and SMAP.

Although the vast majority of Johnny's artists are good-looking young guys with toothsome grins and nice hair, Kitagawa says he has no set formula when putting together his idol-style groups. "It's case by case," says Kitagawa, a Japanese-American who came to Japan with the U.S. Army in the 1950s and who has been here ever since.

The idea for one of his most popular groups, Hikaru Genji, came to him while watching some of his young charges go though their paces during a dancing lesson. "I just asked the boys, 'who's interested in performing on roller skates?' Everybody said 'no: we came here for show business, not roller skating.' But seven guys raised their

V6

SMAP

日本にいなければこのメガポップグループの露出度を感じることは難しいだろう。ジャニーズが90年代中期に送り出してきたSMAPはメディアを独占している。中でも木村拓哉は女性アイドル安室奈美恵とともにその絶大なる人気を誇る。SMAPの人気の高さは96年リリースの『Smappies』（インストルメンタル・カバーアルバム）に参加したオマー・ハキムやウィル・リー等アメリカでもトップのスタジオミュージシャンの驚くべき顔触れを見ても分かる。

hands and said they wanted to do it." The combination of wholesome good looks, ensemble vocals, and roller-skating choreography made Hikaru Genji one of Japan's top acts in the '80s.

Like many long-established agencies, Johnny's main emphasis is on grooming its acts for TV and live performances. To Kitagawa, the show's the thing: not records. "I'm not very interested in records," he states bluntly. "Once you release a record, you have to sell that record. You have to push one song only… You can't think of anything else. It's not good for the artist."

Shonentai, for example, released their first record a full seven years after the group debuted.

Not many Japanese entertainers would think of having their derriere insured. But that's exactly what Shingo Katori, one-fifth of megapopular male vocal/dance idol group SMAP, did in spring 1996. It was part of the publicity buildup for the TV drama series "Toumei

Ningen," in which he had a starring role. Each episode featured at least one scene where Katori flashed some cheek, and each of his buttocks was insured for 100 million yen.

That kind of silliness is par for the course when it comes to SMAP, Japan's biggest idol group in the mid-'90s. SMAP stands for Sports, Music, Assemble, People. Another Johnny's Jimusho act, SMAP started out with twelve members, but as of 1996 was down to five.

If you don't live in Japan, it's hard to appreciate the extent to which the members of a group like SMAP dominate the media — not just the hit charts— when they're in their prime. Take TV commercials. As a group, SMAP at one point was appearing in ads for the telephone company NTT, Lotte sugarless gum, their own "SMAP x SMAP" TV variety show, and the intriguingly named instant and fried noodle Ace Cock.

The group's biggest heartthrob is Takuya Kimura, whose image is almost as

omnipresent in Japan as that of female idol Namie Amuro. SMAP's millions of fans nationwide were devastated in spring 1996 when Katsuyuki Mori announced that he was leaving the group to become a professional motorcycle racer.

One sign of the group's immense popularity in Japan was the 1996 release of the album *SMAPPIES—Rhythmsticks*, which contained instrumental versions of SMAP tunes performed by top-notch American session players such as Omar Hakim, Will Lee, Hiram Bullock, David Spinozza, Mike Mainieri, and the Brecker Brothers. Amazing.

So what about their music? Well, like most Johnny's Jimusho products, the emphasis is on group vocals, with little in the way of harmonizing. The songs are generally uptempo, and in keeping with prevailing trends, the sound is more dance-oriented than that of past idol acts.

They call her "the intelligent idol"—which tells you a lot about the rest of the idol pack. She's Chisato Moritaka, who besides being very good-looking indeed, plays the drums, guitar, and piano. Her long, slender legs are her "charm point," as they say in the idol biz. She's also an accomplished songwriter, which is pretty unusual in the idol field.

Moritaka, who was born in the southern city of Kumamoto in 1969, debuted in 1988. In 1993 illness caused her temporarily to lose her voice, but since then she's made a successful comeback. It's unfair, in a sense, to lump Moritaka in with the rest of Japan's abundant crop of idols, since she is showing signs of outgrowing the idol tag, but Moritaka's visual appeal still features heavily in her promotion. Instead of being a mere puppet like so many idols, she plays an active role in producing her records, playing drums on most tracks, for example, as well as doing her own hair and make-up.

She's also probably the only Japanese idol who would make as unlikely a choice for a song to cover as The Beatles' "Everybody's Got Something to Hide Except Me and My Monkey," which she sang on her 1995 album, *Step by Step*. Moritaka's also got a sly sense of humor, as shown by her track "Rock 'n' Roll Kencho Shozaichi," a culinary tour of the Japanese archipelago set to a '50s-style rock backing.

知的アイドル——そんなレッテルを貼られる森高千里。ルックスに加え、様々な楽器を弾きこなし、そのしなやかな脚はアイドルに欠かせない「チャームポイント」。アイドル的イメージから脱却を図ろうとし、セルフプロデュース部分の多い森高をここで極うのは不公平かもしれないが、ルックスを武器にしていることは事実。しかし、ビートルズのマイナーな曲をカバーしたり、「県所在地ロックンロール」等独特のセンスが光る。

森高千里

CHISATO MORITAKA

PRINCESS PRINCESS

プリンセス²

It's hard to classify an act like Princess Princess, but judging from the extreme devotion shown this five-member female rock band, it's convenient to put them in the idol category.

Ample evidence of that devotion was on display at the group's last-ever concert at Tokyo's Budokan on May 31, 1996. People in their 30s, who'd followed "Pri-pri" ever since the band's 1983 debut were openly, unashamedly weeping. Not too many Japanese rock bands inspire that kind of loyalty.

And not too many manage to stay together as long as Pri-pri did. "It's so difficult to keep a band together," said Shoo Kusano, head of Shinko Music, which managed Princess Princess, after the last show.

The concert was largely a recap of the band's many hits through the years. Princess Princess touched a wide range of stylistic bases: hard rock, pop balladry, an occasional touch of Latin, even country. The five members' appearances ranged from the rather homely Atsuko Watanabe on bass to the rather cute Kaori Okui on lead vocals, while lead guitarist Kanako Nakayama, with her leathers and dyed hair, provided the dash of rock 'n' roll spice the band needed. Pri-pri was a triumph of Japanese pop marketing, and not that bad a band to boot.

In the West, a band's breakup is all too often acrimonious and ugly. In Japan—as exemplified by Pri-pri—it's just another stage in a band's career.

プリンセス・プリンセスのようなバンドを分類するのは難しいが、その熱狂する忠実なファンを見れば容易にアイドルと考えることもできる。96年5月武道館の解散コンサートではデビュー以来のファンはなりふり構わず泣き崩れた。ここまでファンを熱狂させ、なおかつ長続きしたバンドも珍しい。英米ではバンドの解散は苦く醜くなりがちだが、日本ではプリプリのようにバンドキャリアの中の一ステージに過ぎない。

"I don't want to be crushed in the
rush hour until my death
Why, to whom and what do I have
to be tied?
I can see myself struggling in a
stream from which I can't escape."

Yutaka Ozaki The Tragic Idol

Singer-songwriter Yutaka Ozaki is one of Japan's biggest pop idols. His singles sell one-million-plus units. His face regularly graces the pages of Japan's weekly magazines. Ozaki-related goods such as clothes, accessories, and books are hot sellers.

It's a perfect pop success story, except for one problem: Ozaki is dead. Since he died at age 26 on April 25, 1992, Ozaki has become a Japanese folk hero. His story—the rock 'n' roll rebel who followed the path of excess and paid the ultimate price—echoes Japanese history's many tales of doomed heroes who fight against impossible odds and perish in a blaze of glory. Ozaki's death was anything but glorious—he died of excessive accumulation of fluid in his lungs (pulmonary edema) several hours after being found drunk and naked in a Tokyo alley in the early morning. But his ability to express the frustrations of young people chafing under the constraints of a conformist society made him a genuine Japanese rock martyr.

"I don't want to be crushed in the rush hour until my death
Why, to whom and what do I have to be tied?
I can see myself struggling in a stream from which I can't escape."

—"High School Rock 'n' Roll"

Like Kurt Cobain, Ozaki's alienated but articulate lyrics gave voice to the frustrations of thousands of kids who struggle to cope with the madness of the adult world. And unfortunately, like Cobain, Ozaki's escape from that struggle only came with death.

Sony Records, Ozaki's record label, maintains that his death had nothing to do with drug use which, of course, begs the question as to whether alcohol is a drug. But that sort of *tatemae* public facade is greeted with snorts of disbelief by typically cynical music-biz types. The guy got 18 months (suspended) in 1987 for possessing stimulant drugs—speed, or *shabu*, in street Japanese—which historically

has been the illicit drug of choice in fast-paced Japan. That incident affirmed Ozaki's outlaw status, as well as causing him to be dropped by Sony until the company re-signed him in 1990. For hard-core Ozaki fans, there's never been any question of forgetting their hero. His grave in Tokyo's Gokokuji cemetery is a place of pilgrimage. A pedestrian plaza in Tokyo's Shibuya district which Ozaki described as a favorite hangout in a song is another popular spot for Ozaki devotees.

Their holiest of holies, though, is a non-descript house deep in the gray urban sprawl of northeast Tokyo. It belongs to Tadao Komine, a typical hail-fellow-well-met character from Tokyo's *shitamachi*, or working-class district.

After Ozaki's death, fans started placing flowers and other tokens of their regard for Ozaki on the spot where Ozaki was found, which happened to be right beside Komine's house. Komine felt sorry for them, and so he converted one small room of his home into an Ozaki shrine. The walls are covered by photos and fans' drawings of the late star. Some fans have placed bottles of liquor on a table in front of a picture of Ozaki, in keeping with the Japanese tradition in which favorite items of the deceased are left at a grave or Buddhist altar to placate their souls. The fact that alcohol played a large role in Ozaki's demise does not seem to deter them from doing so. "This room is a place for them to be together and remember [Ozaki]," says Komine in an uncharacteristically solemn moment.

"He was honest with us," says Kyoko Hayashi, a high school senior. "In his songs he says what we feel. He was against society and adults who are dirty and aren't honest." Adds Hayashi's 20-year-old sister, Kazumi: "He was different from other pop singers—he sang more than just love songs."

Jロック界の偉大な殉教者、尾崎豊。若くしてこの世を去ったという点を除いて彼の人生は完璧なサクセスストーリーだったといえるだろう。カート・コバーンさながら、排他的かつ歯切れの良い尾崎の歌詞は、汚れきった大人の世界で何とか生き抜こうとあがき苦しむ多くのティーンエイジャーの不満や挫折感を代弁している。そしてコバーン同様、その果てに尾崎を待っていたのは早すぎる死であった。尾崎が倒れ力尽きた東京の路地裏、そのすぐ脇に住む下町気質あふれる小峰氏は、今でも途切れることなく訪れる熱狂的なファンのために、自宅の小さな一室を解放している。壁一面、今は亡きスター、尾崎豊の写真や絵で埋め尽くされた部屋。故人の好物を供えるという仏教の風習がある日本では、ファンが遺影の前にウイスキーのボトルをたむけていく。酒が彼を死に追い込んだという事実は、ファンにとってどうでもよいことのようだ。尾崎豊は疎外や反抗を歌った日本最初のロックシンガーというわけでは決してない。しかし、中でも彼が爆発的な人気を得た理由の一つは、彼がいわゆる政治的な抵抗や反乱を叫んだロッカーではなかったという点だろう。しかし、尾崎ほどのルックスを持ち、かつ妥協無きスタンスでJポップ史に確固たる地位を築いた破滅的な若者はまだいない。彼の激しく哀しげな自己破壊のレガシーは以後のアーチストに多大な影響を与えた。

"On the corner a girl is selling herself, doing anything for money She lost her dream, playing at love, She forgot that she had to let her mind shine all the time. Little by little she is getting to know the meaning of things That have never been taught to her in school."

…from "Seventeen's Map"

Ozaki wasn't the first Japanese rocker to deal with rock's classic themes of alienation and rebellion. Artists such as Panta who came out of the student movement in the late '60s adopted explicitly anti-establishment stances, but they never matched Ozaki's popularity. One reason is that Ozaki's lyrics are not political in the traditional sense.

Ozaki's passionate and sadly self-destructive legacy remains a tough act for other Japanese artists to follow. His rebellion tapped the same wellspring of dissatisfaction beneath the superficial harmony of Japanese society that has inspired more overtly political artists. But no one has said it quite like this handsome, doomed young man whose uncompromising stance gives him a unique place in the history of Japanese pop music:

"I want to break down the door of my feelings, which have no place to go — I don't want to go back to school or home, I want to break down the door of my feelings, which have no place to go – I'm shaking because I can't even know what my existence is."

… from "The Night of 15"

イスラム経典コーランが一部使用されているというクレームによって、ビクターが BUCK TICK のアルバム『Six/Nine』を市場から全面回収したのは95年。民族問題にはかなり敏感な業界でも初めてのことだ。部落問題等に関しては差別用語を排除する為、定期的にマニュアルが配布されている。ジョー・ウォルシュの「Ordinary Average Guy」のアルバム表写真に部落民を意味するジェスチャーが含まれているとし、本国より差し替え用の写真を取り寄せたほど。

It wasn't exactly a Salman Rushdie-type affair, but in 1995 Victor Entertainment became more aware of Moslem sensitivities after adherents of that religion protested the inclusion of a passage from the Koran on an album issued by the label. The protests caused Victor to recall all unsold copies of the album and issue an apology in Japan's major daily newspapers.

The album in question was *Six/Nine*, by rock group Buck-Tick, and the track that caused the controversy was "Rakuen," which translates as "paradise."

"We first became aware of the problem when various Islamic people phoned us up to tell us that a passage from the Koran had been used in 'Rakuen,'" said the Victor A&R director in charge of Buck-Tick. "We were really surprised."

He explained that as far as he knew the Koranic quotation—which he could not identify—was sampled from another recording by one of Buck-Tick's members and mixed into the track.

Victor's apology ad read, in part: "We have inappropriately and inadvertently used, in one of our CDs, a passage from the Islamic holy scripture QURAN [sic], which is not to be used on music, and released it for distribution and sale. We very much regret this incident…"

Very few Moslems live in Japan, and it's a safe bet that most of them are not Buck-Tick fans. Nevertheless, word somehow got out that Islam's holy book had been profaned, and Victor immediately recalled unsold copies of *Six/Nine*, asking those who'd already bought copies to return them in exchange for the new expurgated version.

Wholesalers and record stores returned several tens of thousands of copies of the album, which had initially shipped some 300,000 units. By comparison, the album's new version shipped only some 20,000 copies.

The incident is believed to be the first time a Japanese record company has gotten into hot water over an Islamic-related issue, although Japanese labels are extremely sensitive about offending minority groups.

CULTURAL SENSITIVITIES

Japanese record company employees are routinely issued handbooks listing various verboten expressions and images. Some years back, Sony Records avoided a recall like the one Victor carried out when it discovered that a hand gesture used by guitarist Joe Walsh on the cover of his album Ordinary Average Guy could be construed as a discriminatory reference to the burakumin, an outcast group in feudal Japanese society. Prejudice against burakumin descendants continues in Japanese society, and burakumin groups are quick to draw attention to anything they consider discriminatory.

Industry sources here also say that there are groups specializing in corporate extortion that have no links to minority groups but which play on Japanese companies' fears of messy public confrontations.

In the case of Ordinary Average Guy, Sony asked its counterparts in the United States to supply a new photo for the album's Japanese version.

Pure Pop

Despite the insipid, cookie-cutter nature of much mainstream Japanese pop music, there's actually quite a lot of decent, even brilliant, pop of the classic variety in Japan. It's not rock, it's not dance, it's not enka—it's the kind of stuff where the emphasis is on arrangements, production, catchy melodies, and hooks, as well as solid performances, of course. It's pure pop—lightweight, maybe, but long-lasting.

無味乾燥で判で押したようだと思われがちのJポップにも、実際にはかなりのバラエティがあり、良い意味でクラシックなポップの精神に溢れるサウンドを見つけることができる。ロックでもダンスでも、演歌でもない。アレンジや制作そのものに重きが置かれ、キャッチーなメロディとしっかりとしたパフォーマンス。軽いかもしれないが飽きない。それが純粋なポップ・ミュージックだ。

100%

Like most Japanese female vocalists, Miwa Yoshida is cute. But unlike many of her peers, whose vocal talents take a definite second place to how they score in the looks department, she can sing. A singer's singer, she swoops down from trilling high notes to low, funky phrases with a confidence rarely found in Japanese vocalists—male or female. Yoshida and the two other members of Dreams Come True—bassist/arranger Masato Nakamura and keyboardist Takahiro Nishikawa—have been brightening up the Japanese pop scene since 1988. They released their first album, the self-titled *Dreams Come True* in March 1989, and since then they've become one of Japan's best-loved pop groups.

So far the trio has sold more than 25 million albums and singles, and their 1992 album, The Swinging Star, has sold close to 4 million copies, making it one of the top-selling Japanese albums ever. Tunes like "Sayonara," "Go for it," and "The signs of LOVE" are filled with the kind of catchy hooks that stay in your mind long after the song is over.

In 1995 Yoshida released her first solo album, Beauty and Harmony, an ambitious effort which allowed her to stretch as a vocalist. Backed by leading American session players such as Greg Adams, David T. Walker, and Ralph MacDonald, Yoshida showed a more lowdown, funky side of her musical personality.

One of Yoshida's earliest influences was jazz great Ella Fitzgerald, whom she recalls seeing on TV at the age of 7. "Since that time I've always loved female singers with strong, characteristic voices," she says. DCT is starting to make an impact on the rest of Asia. In 1996, their *Love Unlimited* album sold 200,000 units in Taiwan—just about unheard of for a Japanese act.

Dreams Come True

ヴォーカル吉田美和はキュートなルックスもさることながら、その歌唱力は男女を問わず抜きん出ている。澄んだ高音からファンキーな低音のフレーズまでも見事に歌いこなすそのスタイルは、「日本人離れしている」と言えよう。7歳の時にテレビで見たエラ・フィッツジェラルド等、常に力強い声の女性歌手に憧れてきたという。ベース／アレンジャーの中村正人、キーボード西川隆宏と共に、88年のデビュー以来、最も人気のあるバンドとして日本のポップシーンに君臨し続けている。デビュー以来アルバム、シングルを併せたCDセールスは二千五百万枚余り。四百万枚近く売れた92年リリースの『The Swinging Star』は日本で最も売れたアルバムの一つに数えられている。吉田は95年にソロアルバム『Beauty and Harmony』にも挑戦。ドリカムはアジアにおいても活動を展開。96年リリースの『Love Unlimited』は、台湾では日本人のアルバムとしては異例の十万枚を突破した。

Akiko Yano

Akiko Yano is one of Japan's most original singer/songwriters. Her high-pitched, very feminine vocal style has led some people to compare her to Kate Bush.

Born in 1955, Yano (née Suzuki) started playing piano in jazz clubs while in high school, and released her debut album, Japanese Girl, in 1976. The album was produced by Makoto Yano, whom she married and later divorced, but she's kept the surname Yano. The album featured backing from members of Little Feat and established Yano as a highly original talent. While continuing her solo career, she became associated with Yellow Magic Orchestra on both the personal and professional planes, marrying Ryuichi Sakamoto (they later split up) and touring with YMO in the early '80s. Yano is a superb piano player and a gifted singer, although her little-girl voice isn't to everyone's taste. Her music can be humorous, as in "Ramen Tabetai" ("I Want to Eat Ramen"), but she also has a serious side.

Tatsuro Yamashita

Nobody in Japan is truer to the pure pop ethos than Tatsuro Yamashita. He's a true pop craftsman—a master of melody and the all-important hook. Born in 1953 in Tokyo, Yamashita made his first mark on the music scene in 1975 with the short-lived but influential band Sugar Babe. In 1976 he went solo, and released a series of critically praised but poor-selling albums. He finally made it big with his fifth solo effort, 1979's *Moonglow*, which stayed on the charts for 50 weeks.

In 1991 he released one of his best albums, *Artisan*, which included three singles that charted as well as an inspired remake of the Four Freshmen's "New York's a Lonely Town" (retitled "Tokyo's a Lonely Town"), which he sang convincingly in English.

ポップの精神に最も忠実なメロディメーカー山下達郎。75年に、短命ながら後のJポップシーンに多大な影響を残したバンド、シュガーベイブに在籍。76年ソロデビュー。91年ベストアルバム『Artisan』ではフォー・フレッシュメンの曲を見事な英語でカバー。Jポップシーンで最もオリジナリティのある女性シンガーソングライター、和製ケイト・ブッシュたる矢野顕子。ピアニストだけでなく歌の評価も高いが、少女のようなソプラノは好みが別れるところ。

Great 3

Taking Japanese pop to new heights of melodious sophistication are the Great 3, whose second album, Metal Lunchbox, was one of the best things to happen on the Japanese music scene in 1996. The band was formed in 1994 when guitarist Akito Katayose, bassist Kiyoshi Takakuwa, and drummer Kenichi Shirane, who collectively had been one-half of the band Rotten Hats, left that band to form the Great 3. Katayose, who writes most of the band's material, addresses topics such as man's indecisiveness in the face of love. The sound of the Great 3 is reminiscent of the High Llamas at times, but with much more of a power-pop punch.

Mariya Takeuchi

日本のポップを新しい次元へと昇華させた Great 3 のセカンドアルバム『Metal Lunchbox』は 96 年 J ポップ最高の作品。彼等の音は時として High Llamas を彷彿させるがさらにパンチが効いている。竹内まりやは 84 年以来ライブ活動もテレビ出演もしていないが安定した人気を誇るトップアーティスト。81 年に結婚、長い活動を停止するもののカムバック。夫の山下達郎同様、彼女の音楽も王道を行く聞きやすいポップなメロディが特徴。

Mariya Takeuchi has not performed live since 1981. She hasn't appeared on TV since 1984. Yet Mariya Takeuchi is one of Japan's most consistently popular female singer/songwriters.

After her debut in 1978, Takeuchi followed the conventional idol career path. But in 1981, illness caused her to take a break from the fast-paced pop world. She then married singer/songwriter Tatsuro Yamashita, and settled down to the domestic life, releasing the comeback album *Variety* in 1984. Takeuchi's style, like that of her husband, is lush, classic pop. And like Yamashita, one single of Takeuchi's gets loads of airplay in Japan come Christmas: Takeuchi's version (produced by Yamashita) of the seasonal classic "The Christmas Song."

37

It's tempting to call Chage and Aska the Wham! of Japan, but like similar analogies, it just doesn't work. While it's true that like Wham!, one guy has it all in the looks department while the other ... er ... doesn't, the Japanese duo is much more of an equal musical partnership than many other two-man acts. Their music is slick pop, with the polished sheen Japanese producers like. For most of their fans, Chage and Aska's main attraction is Aska's soulful and adult-sounding voice. Chage and Aska's biggest impact came in the early '90s, when they played a major role in ushering in the megahits era with million-selling singles like "Say Yes" and albums such as *Tree.* In 1996 they became the first Asian act to do an MTV "Unplugged" session.

Chage & Aska

ルックスは日本版ワム！と呼びたくなるCHAGE&ASKA。だが音楽面ではこの比喩はあてはまらない。シャープな音作り、ソウルフルなASKAのヴォーカルが魅力だ。90年代初期『Say Yes』等によりメガヒット時代の立役者となった。ジャンルに捕われないdip in the poolはプロデューサー／キーボート／プログラミングの木村達司と元モデルのヴォーカル甲田益也子のユニット。85年のデビュー以来、不思議な魅力に溢れた音楽を作り続けている。

Dip in the pool is one of many Japanese pop acts that's pretty well unclassifiable. A collaboration between Tatsuji Kimura (producer/keyboards/programming) and vocalist Miyako Koda, the "dips" have been putting out quirky but appealing music since their 1985 debut. Another example of a great Japanese pop unit that deserves far greater exposure, especially since Koda (a one-time fashion model) sings in English as well as Japanese. Koda was one of the three female singers (along with Mimori Yusa and Mishio Ogawa) on Haruomi Hosono's excellent 1995 album *Love, Peace and Trance.*

dip in the pool

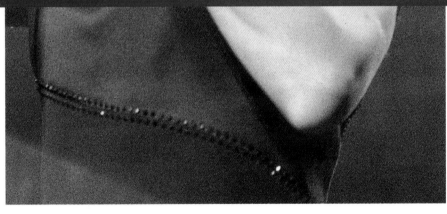

中島みゆきは、シンガーソングライター、ラジオDJ、詩人、小説家と広い活動で、アジア女性の持つステレオタイプなイメージ（西太后的な独裁者のイメージと、その一方でセックスシンボルとしての弱々しくコケティッシュなイメージ）を打ち壊し、よりポジティブな女性像を表現。彼女の音楽はポップなメロディーとロックのパワフルさを器用にミックスし、繊細な歌詞はシャンソンを思わせる。「夜会」と呼ばれるコンサートは他の追従を許さない。

The two classic stereotypical images of Asian women are the manipulative, powerful Dragon Lady and the demure, submissive sex kitten. Offering a much more positive role model for Japanese women than either of those clichéd images is Miyuki Nakajima—singer/songwriter, radio personality, poet, and novelist. Her music is a deft combination of the melodiousness of pop and the power of rock, and manages to avoid the extremes of both genres.

Melodramatic and melancholic are words that come to mind when describing Nakajima's musical and lyrical sensibility. Think chanson. Nakajima's been a mainstay on the Japanese entertainment scene since winning the Grand Prix at Yamaha's World Popular Song Festival in 1975. Her albums, which come out each October, are steady sellers. Unlike most Japanese pop stars, Nakajima almost never makes TV appearances.

Besides regular concerts, Nakajima stays in the public eye with her annual Yakai (soirée) concerts, which combine music and spectacle in an imaginative way that leaves the stage presentations of other pop stars way behind.

Her Yakai series (which usually comprises 23 or so performances) is immensely popular. Tickets for all the shows sell out in an hour. Before each show—held at Tokyo's 747-seat Theatre Cocoon—scalpers (known as *dafuya* in Japanese) ask as much as ¥50,000 for ¥9,000 tickets.

No Japanese singer sweats as much as Keisuke Kuwata. In concert, the Southern All Stars' lead vocalist is a plethora of perspiration. That hard-working style is one reason why SAS is the all-time top-selling rock band in Japanese music history: since the band was formed in 1975, they've sold 22.5 million singles and 23 million albums. Their first big hit came in 1978 with the Kuwata composition "Nagisa no Shindobatto" ("Seaside Sinbad"). Other SAS hits through the years have included "Itoshi-no-Elly" in 1979 (which was a big hit in Japan for Ray Charles as "Ellie My Love"), "Bye Bye My Love" in 1985, "Minna no Uta" in 1987, "Sayonara Baby" in 1990, "Erotica Seven" in 1993, and the unfortunately titled "Mampy no G-spot" in 1995.

A key part of the band's appeal is Kuwata's unique singing style: most Japanese will tell you that he sings Japanese as if the words were English. One possible reason for the band's longevity is that SAS keyboardist/vocalist Yuko Hara is also Kuwata's wife. For all his on-stage looning about, Kuwata is actually a serious guy. When the Japanese music community started the Act Against AIDS campaign in 1993, Kuwata read everything he could get his hands on concerning the disease so that he could speak with authority to audiences attending the campaign's various events.

桑田佳祐ほど汗まみれに歌うシンガーも珍しい。その一生懸命さがサザンを日本の音楽シーンを常にリードし、トップの売り上げを誇るロックバンドにしているのかもしれない。桑田のあたかも英語で歌っているかのような独特のヴォーカルスタイルはファンを魅了。キーボード原由子は桑田の妻、結成以来不動のメンバーを維持している。ステージではおどけて見せる桑田だが、93年にはエイズ防止チャリティキャンペーンを展開した。

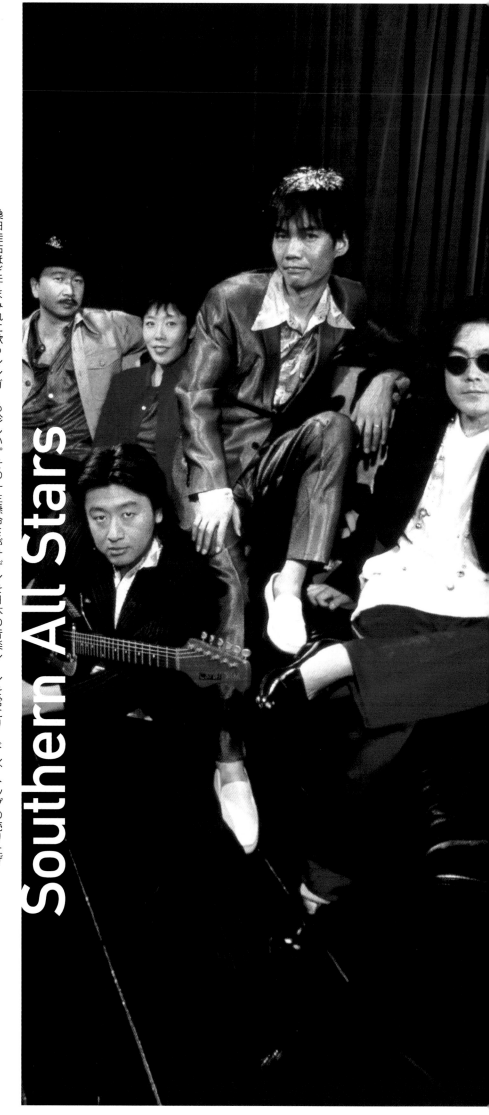

Southern All Stars

One of the biggest dates on the Japanese pop world's calendar is the late November release of "Yuming's" annual album, which is always launched with a huge publicity campaign.

Matsutoya's image of the self-reliant, mature woman helps makes her a favorite among young working women. Her music is characterized by its smooth, West Coast sound and her immediately recognizable voice—which you either love or hate. Matsutoya, who is married to producer Masataka Matsutoya, is also known for her elaborate, high-tech stage shows.

Yumi Matsutoya

aka Yuming

日本のポップミュージックカレンダーで重要な日の一つに、11月末のユーミン新譜発売日がある。それは毎年一大キャンペーンとともにやって来る。彼女の独立心に長けた成熟したイメージが働く女性達に愛される理由だ。松任谷の滑らかな音楽はウエストコーストサウンドに近く、好き嫌いはともかく特徴ある声は彼女のそれとすぐ分かる。松任谷正隆の妻でもあり、ハイテクを駆使した豪華なステージでも知られている。

Takeshi Kobayashi & My Little Lover

小室哲哉と並びプロデューサーの位置を高めた小林武史。彼のプロデューサーとしてのブレイクはMy Little Lover。『Now and Then』のような曲は『Magical Mystery Tour』時代のビートルズを彷彿させる美しいメロディーと綿密なレコーディングを可能にする小林の高い能力の表れだ。小泉今日子やチャラをプロデュースする一方、Yen Town Bandの名で制作の映画スワロウテイルのサントラ『Montage』は見事な出来。

Along with dance/pop wizard Tetsuya Komuro, Takeshi Kobayashi has brought the role of the producer to the forefront of Japanese pop. In big demand as a freelance producer, he first made his mark with the three-person "unit" My Little Lover (MLL), whose other two members are guitarist Kenji Fujii and ethereal vocalist Akko. Kobayasho's ability to construct three-minute pop symphonies is apparent on MLL tracks like "Now and Then," whose beautiful melodies and intricate production values recall the high psychedelia of the Beatles' Magical Mystery Tour period. Other artists Kobayashi has worked with include idol singer Kyoko Koizumi and, most recently, Lolita-voiced chanteuse Chara, with whom he made the excellent soundtrack album *Montage* under the name Yen Town Band.

Mr. Children

These two bands, which both qualify for inclusion in Japanese pop's rather large "shame about the name" department, specialize in melodic, mid-'60s-U.K.-flavored pop. Spitz hit it big in 1995 with the song "Robinson," as their brand of pleasant pop won over Japanese music fans. What makes Spitz special is Masamune Kusano's boyish voice, which resonates with the *natsukashii* ("nostalgic," "wistful," and "longed-for" are rough approximations) quality that makes Japanese go all dewy-eyed.

Mr. Children's hits include "Everybody Goes," which has sold more than 1.2 million copies since its November 1994 release, and their 1995 album, *Atomic Heart*. The band's producer is the very successful Takeshi Kobayashi.

Jポップには恥ずかしい名前を持つバンドが少なくないのだが、この二つのバンドもその中に含まれるだろう。彼等の音楽はメロディアスな60年中期の英国系ポップサウンド。95年に「ロビンソン」でブレイクしたスピッツはどこか懐かしくキュンとなる草野マサムネの少年のような声にその魅力がある。小林武史がプロデュースするMr. Childrenはアルバム『Everybody Goes』が120万枚売れ、95年に『Atomic Heart』をリリースしている。

Spitz

85年に渋谷ライブインで米米CLUBを見たのが私にとって日本で初のライブ体験だった。そのキザでテンポ良くユーモア溢れるステージに、このバンドは売れると思った。現実その通りとなり、Jポップ界でも屈指のバンドとなった。サウンドはサザン等よりもR&Bファンク色に富む。97年に解散すると発表され、その長く輝かしい成功に一応の幕を降ろすが、伊達男カールスモーキー石井やジェームス小野田は必ず違う形で我々の前に戻ってくるだろう。

Kome Kome Club

Kome Kome (which means "rice, rice") Club (KKC) was the first band I ever saw in Japan, way back in 1985 at the long-defunct (and very cramped) Shibuya Live Inn. With their hyper-slick, fast-paced, tight, and very funny show, it was obvious they were heading straight for the big time. And that's exactly what happened, as they became one of Japan's biggest and most consistently successful pop acts. There was much more of an R&B/funk edge to their music than with, say, the Southern All Stars, and their sometimes bombastic tendencies were balanced by their tongue-in-cheek sensibility.

Front man Carl "Smokey" Ishii's macho posturing was just slightly over-the-top, and his theatrical approach carried over to the band's stage design and costumes—KKC was a very visual band, and they put on one of the best live shows in Japan.

In late 1996 they announced they would split up in March 1997, which brought to an end one of Japanese pop's longest-running success stories. But we're sure to be hearing more from Ishii, James Onoda, and the rest of the KKC crew.

ポップ・ミュージック界で注目すべきこれからのシンガーにUAがいる。(UAとはスワヒリ語で「花」・「殺す」と言う二つの意味
っている。)数人のプロデューサーが関わってできた96年リリースデビューアルバム『11』はクラブ、ソウル、エスニック等様々
いジャンルの曲で構成されている。全てに唯一共通しているのは、他の女性シンガーとは一線を画す彼女の深くセクシーな歌
ろう。これからが期待される。

UA
u:ah

One of Japan's most intriguing female
singers is newcomer UA (the name is a
Swahili word that means "flower" or
"kill"). Her 1996 debut album, *11*, covers a
wide variety of stylistic bases, including
club, soul, and "ethnic," and featured
various well-known producers. The one
constant is UA's deep, seductive voice,
which immediately sets her apart from
other Japanese female singers. Someone
to watch out for.

UA means "flower" or "kill"

45

Most Japanese pop, whether it's the bubblegum fare of terminally cute teenage idol singers or the darkest, dankest underground noise, is Western in the sense that it uses Western instruments—guitars, pianos, and the like as well as a Western musical scale.

Some Japanese musicians, however, make an effort to use homegrown rhythms and instruments to give their music an ethnic flavor. Sometimes the results are tokenistic crap; other times the results are very interesting indeed.

One pioneering attempt to use Japanese musical forms in a pop context was Osamu Kitajima's 1975 album *Benzaiten*, which blended electric guitars and traditional Japanese instruments like the biwa lute, shakuhachi flute, and koto. In the early '90s there was a rock group called Ajyota whose gimmick was to use nothing but modified and amplified Japanese instruments. Bass samisen, anyone?

That kind of attempted East-West fusion aside, it's not uncommon for Japanese pop/rock to include the odd bit of samisen or shakuhachi to give a song a Japanese vibe. People like Yellow Magic Orchestra alumnus Ryuichi Sakamoto often add a dash of Okinawan *sanshin* (a three-stringed instrument similar to mainland Japan's samisen, but featuring a shorter neck and snakeskin instead of cat or dog skin strung over the resonance box), for example, to their recordings. But only a handful of Japanese groups have managed to update traditional musical forms and put them in a more contemporary context without sounding gimmicky or bogus.

Foremost among them is Champloose, led by Shoukichi Kina, one of the most respected figures in the Japanese music world. Champloose's unique sound is based on a combination of the sanshin and electric instruments. The group's first big hit was 1974's "Haisai Ojisan," a bright, happy pop tune that always gets the crowd dancing at Champloose's

typically exuberant concerts. Highly recommended is the group's 1980 album, *Blood Line*, which includes the ballad "Subete no Hito no Kokoro ni Hana wo" ("Flowers for Every Heart"), usually referred to simply as "Hana." This beautiful song has been covered countless times, including many versions by other Asian artists. It occupies a place in Japanese pop analogous to that of "Yesterday" in the Western pop canon.

Besides writing great songs, Kina has done more than any other person to popularize Okinawan music in mainland Japan. A genuine Japanese eccentric, Kina has been leading various incarnations of Champloose since the late '70s. Kina is as much shaman as showman, as he exhorts his audience to loosen up and get into the matsuri (festival) spirit he tries to create at his shows.

Playing either sanshin or electric guitar, Kina's impassioned vocals work the audience up into a frenzy as a chorus of female singers chant *hai-ya, hai-ya, hai-ya, iya-sasa* to a typically frenetic Okinawan beat. Frustrated with the way Japanese record companies had handled his career, Kina took an extended sabbatical through most of the '80s. In 1990 he released a brilliant comeback album, *Nirakanai Paradise*, which coincided with a resurgence of interest in Japanese roots music.

Since then he's taken all sorts of stylistic detours in his effort to put a new spin on Okinawan music. For example, Champloose's 1991 album, *Earth Spirit*, partly recorded in Paris with musicians from France, Cameroon, and Martinique, successfully combined Okinawan sounds with the up-tempo *zouk* music of the Caribbean.

アイドル歌手にしろ、カルト的バンドにしろ、洋楽器を使用する限り日本の殆どのポップ・ミュージックは洋楽と言えるだろう。しかし中には日本古来独特の音楽、楽器を取り入れ民族的オリジナリティを出そうと努力するアーチスト達もいる。結果は様々。上っ面だけのものもあれば、時として興味深い音を醸し出す。75年喜多島修のアルバム「弁才天」では琵琶、尺八、琴がポップ・ミュージックに取り入れられた。しかしながら伝統音楽を効果的に取り入れることに成功しているケースはまだまだ少ない。その数少ない中の代表が日本音楽界でも尊敬される存在の喜納昌吉が率いるチャンプルーズ。三線とエレクトリック楽器を組合わせたスタイル。代表曲「花」は多くのアーティストにカバーされ、日本の『Yesterday』的存在。喜納の功績は優れた曲作りのみならず、沖縄音楽の普及にある。91年にはパリでカリブのアーティスト達とレコーディングを行っている。

Interviewing Shoukichi Kina is like trying to carry on three or four conversations at once, as his quicksilver mind darts laterally from topic to topic and from Okinawan dialect to standard Japanese to English.

What's the difference between Japanese and Okinawan music?

There is a different style of playing in Japan and Okinawa. Okinawa has more energy. Sanshin music is very upbeat and can easily reach people's hearts. When people listen to sanshin music, they start dancing pretty quickly. But Japanese samisen music is more philosophical—almost sad.

Some people in Okinawa say you're not playing real Okinawan music...

Everyone says that. Okinawan people believe in a very traditional musical style. They hate me. So my fans are young people. I believe Okinawan music has to change. That's why I wrote "Haisai Ojisan." It's kind of Okinawan pop music.

What's your family background?

My father has a music store. I was one of five children. Then my father married again, so finally there were 11 children. I thought I was different from other children. I didn't learn music from my father, but my brothers and sisters did. My father knew I had a special power, so he didn't interfere with me. I knew I would learn anyway. I'm the eldest. Our family has a strong connection with shamanism.

Are you a shaman?

I don't think I'm a shaman, but I can understand shamanism. But I am a kind of medium because I can understand (these things) very well. You may have heard that I am crazy but I'm not—I'm just a messenger. The spirit controls my body.

Over the years you've played many concerts with Ainu musicians. What's the connection between Ainu music and Okinawan music?

I want to make one spirit in Japan. I want to recreate human nature through music. It's all one heart, one spirit. I've seen lots of racism against Ainu and day laborers in San'ya (a rundown Tokyo district) They need my help so they invite me to play. I want the minorities and the majority of Japan to make contact through music. Japan is the balance of West and East. Japan is the most important meeting place in this area.

喜納昌吉へのインタビューはまるで数人と同時に会話をしているようだ。彼の鋭い感性は、トピックからトピックへ、沖縄弁から標準語そして英語へと縦横無尽に移り渡る。〈日本と沖縄音楽の違いは？〉沖縄三線は明るく思わず踊り出したくなるが、和三味線は物哀しい。〈本当の琉球音楽ではないという意見については？〉沖縄人はとても保守的で私の音楽を嫌っている。でもそれを変えて行かなければ。だから沖縄ポップ「ハイサイおじさん」を作った。〈音楽的背景〉父が楽器店を経営。11人兄弟の長男だった私はどこか自分自身でも何か特別な力を持っていると思っていたし、父もそれを分かってくれていた。だから私に音楽を教えようとはしなかった。家系的にはシャーマニズムと深い繋がりがあった。私はシャーマンではないが、霊と人を結ぶメッセンジャーだ。〈アイヌとの交流〉全ての日本人が一つになれるように、彼等の助けとなりたい。日本は西と東が出会う重要な所だから。

48

a chat with **Kina**

最も興味深いバンドの一つ、上々颱風。彼等の音は日本民謡と沖縄のメロディー、チャイニーズとロックのミックスに時としてブルースも加わる。7人編成バンドの中心はリーダー紅龍と2人の女性ヴォーカル。スキンヘッドにサングラス、真っ赤なつなぎという出で立ちの紅龍の型破りさはバンジョーに三味線の弦を張るというスタイルにも表われている。アメリカンロックや日本のフォークを聴いて育った彼は、日本人の肌に最も良く合う伝統的な日本のリズムが何故もっと使われないのかが不思議だと言う。緩急うまく織り混ぜた上々颱風のライブは素晴らしく、ほろ苦い過去の恋を秋刀魚の味に例える「秋刀魚の唄」は秀逸。

Shang Shang Typhoon

One of the most interesting bands in Japan today has the unlikely name of Shang Shang Typhoon. This six-member group's music draws on traditional Japanese folk songs, as well as melodies from Okinawa, Chinese songs, plus a liberal dash of rock and even an occasional nod to the blues. The band, fronted by female vocalists Satoko Nishikawa and Emi Shirosaki, has existed in various forms since 1980, when it was founded by the enigmatic Koryu ("red dragon").

Koryu is definitely not your average Japanese salaryman, what with his shaven head, dark sunglasses, and red overalls. His unconventional style extends to his choice of instrument: a banjo strung with the strings of the traditional three-stringed samisen.

Koryu says this hybrid creation is easier to play for someone like him with no formal training in traditional Japanese music.

"I grew up listening to American rock, but I also listened to Japanese folk songs," he says. "I wondered why Japanese pop music couldn't use traditional rhythms, which most Japanese people are familiar with. The melodies suit Japanese people."

Until 1990 the band stayed out of the limelight, playing at events like local festivals instead of the usual concert hall circuit. But with the release of their eponymous first album in April 1990 on Epic/Sony, the word was out: Shang Shang Typhoon were Japanese and weren't afraid to flaunt it.

Shang Shang Typhoon is one of the best live acts in Japan. Nishikawa and Shirosaki, in their brightly colored flowing robes, alternate between energetic, high-pitched vocals during uptempo numbers and delicate, beautifully phrased singing for slower songs, while Koryu leads the rest of the band—bass, drums, keyboards, percussion—his banjo-cum-samisen setting the pace.

Their music isn't based on any particular Japanese or Asian style. Instead it draws on a wide range of influences. One of their more unusual tunes is a folksy, Japanese-language version of the Beatles' "Let It Be."

Most of Shang Shang Typhoon's songs, however, are written by Koryu, whose deft way with melodies and lyrics makes him one of Japan's best contemporary songwriters. Typical of his subtle touch is a tune called "Sanma no Uta," in which a woman describes how the smell of *sanma* (swordfish; literally "autumn sword") being fried reminds her of a love affair she had the previous autumn. The song compares sanma's somewhat bitter taste with the bitterness of love. That's a very Japanese metaphor that's quite effective.

Nenes

三味線プレイヤー・知名定男の生徒だった4人の女性コーラス・ネーネーズには思わず聴いてしまう暖かさが溢れ、比較的とっつき安いだろう。92年リリースされたメジャーデビューアルバム「ユンタ」中の沖縄弁バージョンの『Banana Boat Song』は必聴。

ネーネーズ

Somewhat more acceptable to purists is the music of four-woman choral group the Nenes (pronounced "nay nays"), even though they throw in a few offbeat cover versions on their albums just to keep things interesting. Former students of sanshin player Sadao China, the Nenes have an irresistible downhome style that's less in-your-face than Kina or Rinken.

The Nenes were formed under China's auspices in 1990, and in 1992 they made their major-label debut with the excellent album *Yunta*. One of the highlights of that album was their amazing, Ryukyu-dialect version of the "Banana Boat Song" (you know, the one with the "Day-O!" chorus).

"We got the idea for (using that song) because the album (was) called *Yunta*, which means 'work song'," explained lead vocalist Misako Koja.

Their third album, *Ashibi* (a Ryukyu word which roughly translates as playing or relaxing), included traditional songs such as "Akabana," pop tunes like "Bye Bye Okinawa," and a haunting cover of Bob Marley's "No Woman, No Cry."

"Young people in Okinawa show no interest in traditional music," says Koja, who was a member the backing chorus for Ryuichi Sakamoto during one of his tours. "China-san decided on this means in order to attract their attention."

Besides Champloose, another Okinawan band to have achieved some degree of popularity in the rest of Japan is the Rinken Band. More theatrical in approach than Champloose, the elaborately costumed members of the Rinken Band complement their music with choreography, jokes, and stories. Audiences seem to enjoy this, but the atmosphere at their concerts is more restrained than at a Champloose gig.

The band's leader, Teruya Rinken, comes from a musical family in Okinawa, and like Kina he is fiercely proud of Okinawan culture. He says that although his band uses Western instruments like bass, drums, and synthesizers, they are used in an Okinawan context, just as the sanshin, which originated in China, was earlier adapted by the Okinawans.

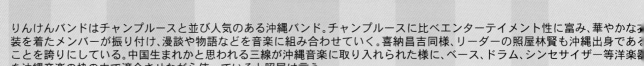

りんけんバンドはチャンプルースと並び人気のある沖縄バンド。チャンプルースに比べエンターテイメント性に富み、華やかな衣装を着たメンバーが振り付け、漫談や物語などを音楽に組み合わせていく。喜納昌吉同様、リーダーの照屋林賢も沖縄出身であることを誇りにしている。中国生まれかと思われる三線が沖縄音楽に取り入れられた様に、ベース、ドラム、シンセサイザー等洋楽器を沖縄音楽の枠の中で適合させながら使っていると照屋は言う。

Rinken Band

Soul Flower Union

Although not usually thought of as an "ethnic" band in the same way as Shang Shang Typhoon or Champloose, neo-psychedelic group Soul Flower Union (SFU) draws heavily on traditional Japanese and other Asian sounds in forging its uniquely powerful music. You could call it ethno-psychedelia, with a heavy dollop of socio-political awareness thrown in for good measure.

SFU was formed in 1993 with the merger of two bands: Newest Model and the provocatively named Mescaline Drive. From the beginning, SFU has maintained a militantly anti-establishment stance. In the song "Dance Your Village's Original Dance," they described the oppression suffered over the centuries by the Ainu at the hands of the majority Yamato Japanese:

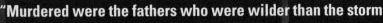

**"Murdered were the fathers who were wilder than the storm
And stronger than the silver mountains
Taken away were the mothers' lives
More generous than the river ....
We dig a hole called 'assimilation'
And bury them all alive."**

Few Japanese rock groups are ever as politically outspoken as this.

"The Japanese government forced the Ainu people to adopt Japanese culture. I hope this song inspires our audience to restudy Ainu issues as part of the history of our country," comments SFU vocalist/guitarist Takashi Nakagawa, who co-wrote "Dance" with fellow band member Hideko Itami. "This society doesn't accept things or people that are different from what's 'normal,' such as handicapped people," he says.

Nakagawa is quick to deny that SFU is a "message" band.

"It's dangerous to be labeled like that," he notes. "We formed this band to see what kind of sound the six of us would create as an ensemble. It's like a tiny society," Nakagawa explains, adding that it's natural for the band

members' social concerns to come up in the songs they write.

On their 1996 album, *Electro Asyl-Bop*, SFU's fusion of militancy and roots music was fully realized in songs like "Eejynaika (Nevermind)":

"… Oh, the pitiful fruitless chess pawn. Nevermind about winning or losing. Nevermind the Emperor!"

The song, which was inspired by an anti-feudal revolt in the last years of the Edo period (1603-1867), uses traditional instruments such as the Japanese *wadaiko* and Korean *chung* drums, as well as the electric sitar (played by Tokyo Bibimbap Club's Hirofumi Kasuga, who guests on several of the album's tunes) to create a raucous, folksy feeling.

The "ethnic" side of SFU is most apparent on the deeply moving "Mangetsu no Yube" ("Full Moon Evening"), which features a powerful lead vocal by Nakagawa (who also plays Okinawan sanshin) and an assortment of Japanese and Korean traditional instruments.

上々颱風やチャンプルースのようにあからさまにエスニック系という訳ではないが、ネオ・サイケバンドとも言うべきソウル・フラワー・ユニオン(SFU)も日本の伝統的音楽とアジアサウンドの影響を強く受け、類まれなパワフルな音楽を展開している。アイヌ問題に触発された曲を作るなど社会的な一面もある。江戸末期の一揆騒動にインスピレーションを受けた「ええじゃないか」ではアイヌ問題に触発された曲を作るなど社会的な一面もある。和太鼓、チンドン太鼓、シタール等をフィーチャーした。

While more mainland Japanese are becoming aware of Okinawa's musical heritage, that of the Ainu, the aboriginal inhabitants of northern Honshu and Hokkaido, is still pretty obscure. The Ainu culture has almost totally disappeared due to racism and assimilation, and Shoukichi Kina, for one, has incorporated elements of their music into his recordings as part of his effort to make Japan's majority culture more tolerant and respectful of minorities like the Ainu and the Okinawans.

An interesting attempt to update the Ainu musical heritage was a 1991 private release, *Kamuychikap* (God's Bird), by a group of Ainu and Japanese musicians known collectively as Moshiri. Several of the tunes feature the *mukkuri*, an Ainu instrument which sounds like a jew's harp, as well as beautiful, haunting vocals in the Ainu language.

The leader of Moshiri is a charismatic chap whose Japanese name is Masanori Toyooka, but who prefers to use his Ainu name, Atuy. He was exposed to traditional Ainu music in his childhood through his grandparents. At age 16 he went overseas and learned about various ethnic groups such as North American Indians. Although he's been influenced by many different types of music, Ainu culture remains the basis of his music.

He's an outspoken advocate of Ainu culture and self-determination.

"They (the Japanese) think we are ignorant and uneducated, that we are inferior to wajin (Japanese). When they see us, they think we are not human. They think we have a low level of culture. Such a way of thinking hurts us. Even now it's like this."

"We don't want to work for a big (record) company, because their policy is just to make a profit, but I want to do a good job. The purpose of our music is to make an environment in which human beings and nature can co-exist, and all peoples in the world—Japanese, French, African, American, whatever— can become friends and we can all help each other. We call this respect for different cultures."

The standout track on *Kamuychikap* is an Ainu lullaby titled "Ihunke," whose haunting refrain stays with you long after the song has ended.

沖縄音楽に対する意識が高まる中、本州の最北部から北海道にかけての先住民族アイヌの音楽はまだまだマイナーな扱いを受けている。差別と同化によってアイヌ文化は壊滅的な状態となってしまったが、喜納昌吉らによってその要素を徐々にメジャー領域に取り入れていこうとする動きはある。アイヌ音楽を現代的にアレンジする試みの代表格がモシリ。91年にはプライベートレーベルから印象深い「カムイチカプ」をリリースしている。

アイヌ

In the early '90s, a short-lived but fascinating Tokyo-based band called Voice From Asia took "ethnic" music in a unique, experimental direction. The sound of the quirky yet fascinating five-piece group was dominated by Shizuru Ohtaka's unique voice, which ranges from the sultry to the strident and various points in between. Ohtaka sang in Japanese, French, and often in her own private language (think of the Cocteau Twins' Elizabeth Fraser), while the rest of the band played an unusual combination of avant-garde stylings and Asian melodies and rhythms.

Ironically, Voice From Asia used no Asian instruments—unless you count the Japanese children's toys from which Ohtaka extracted various beeps, whistles, and squeals.

"We were tired of American music," says band leader Ichiyo Kishimoto, who alternated between violin and mandolin. "I wasn't a great player, but I wanted to do something different."

Ohtaka, who grew up listening to traditional minyo songs and later studied Western classical music and jazz, is equally modest about her musical abilities. "I like to listen to minyo, but it's difficult to actually play it or sing it," she points out.

Voice From Asia broke up after releasing one CD, but since then Ohtaka has released a series of fascinating, off-the-wall albums that have caused more than a few people to claim she is Japan's best female vocalist.

Ohtaka makes her living by recording vocals for TV and radio commercials. "I like singing commercial songs in the studio," she said in a 1994 interview, "because it's like a craftsperson's work. It's really difficult to make company or product names sound impressive and in tune, but it really helps me to brush up my singing ability."

Her first foray into the professional musical world came when she was attending college. A friend suggested that Ohtaka, who had been singing backing vocals on an amateur basis, audition for an automobile ad. She did, and to her surprise, she got the job.

Later, to pay the rent, she worked as an international telephone operator, which helped her hone her linguistic skills.

Besides her solo albums, Ohtaka has recorded a couple albums with a unit called "dido," on the first of which sax player Wayne Shorter was a featured guest. On *ksana*, dido took the form of a two-person unit comprised of Ohtaka and Michiaki Kato, a talented guitarist/keyboardist who is the perfect musical foil for Ohtaka's vocal explorations. Their music transcends national and cultural boundaries, while freely taking elements from various cultures' music, and integrating them into something new and different.

Ohtaka is nothing if not eclectic: she's played with Sudanese lute player Hamza Eldeen and provided backing vocals for a performance by *butoh* dancer Kazuo Ohno, as well as covering material ranging from "Amazing Grace" to Shoukichi Kina's "Hana." She remains someone to watch on the Japanese music scene.

静
流

Shizuru Ohtaka

Okinawa: Japan's Deep South

Culturally and geographically, Okinawa is Japan's Deep South. It's one place where roots music is a vital part of contemporary culture, unlike mainland Japan, which in large part has lost touch with its folk heritage. In fact, Okinawan music sounds so exotic to the average Japanese that in Japanese record stores it's usually found in the World Music section—not in the Japanese *hogaku* (Japanese domestic music) section.

At the heart of Okinawan music is the timeless sound of the sanshin. Wherever you are in Okinawa, in downtown Naha, or in a tiny village in one of the outlying islands, odds are you'll hear the instrument's distinctive plink-a-plunk sound. A sanshin player is never in a hurry. The notes drift out of the three-stringed instrument at a leisurely, almost erratic pace that suits the mood and ambience of these relaxed islands.

The sanshin isn't native to Okinawa, but comes from China, like so much of Ryukyu (and Japanese) culture. From Okinawa the sanshin moved north to Amami Island, south of Kyushu, and then to Kagoshima in Kyushu. In mainland Japan the sanshin evolved into the samisen, which has a longer neck than the sanshin.

Chofuku Terukina, a resident of the main island of Okinawa who's been making sanshins for 40 years, explains that to make a proper instrument, you've got to use snakeskin. (Besides being longer, the mainland Japanese instrument is made with cat skin, and uses a different scale.) Terukina has no time for synthetic material.

"Snakeskin has a better sound," says Terukina, who gets the dried skins from Thailand. The other material necessary for making a good sanshin is ebony, preferably from trees 200 to 300 years old. There aren't many left in Okinawa, so most of the ebony Terukina uses comes from the Philippines.

Top-end sanshins go for over ¥3 million apiece. One of Terukina's garden-variety sanshins, by comparison, can cost as little as ¥30,000.

"It takes 15 days to make one sanshin," says Terukina, "but it takes 20 years to learn how to make one. And to make a good sanshin, you've got to play the instrument well." And he does, turning his small, cluttered office into a concert hall by giving an impromptu performance. The instrument's high, pure tones contrast with Terukina's deep, resonant voice.

He recommends a trip down to Ishigaki island, center of the traditional yaeyama style of sanshin music, to hear the music at its source.

The pace of life on Ishigaki is even more laid-back than on the main island of Okinawa, and the tropical ambience is stronger. Sitting in the living room of sanshin teacher Choden Tamayose, munching away at *imokuzuandaagi*, a reddish-purple potato cooked in tempura batter, the urban madness of Tokyo seems very far away indeed.

Tamayose says that after the war Okinawans began to have more leisure time, and as a result the sanshin's popularity grew tremendously. "Now everybody plays it."

Tamayose is a proselytizer for the sanshin. "Playing the sanshin cures all suffering and relieves tiredness," he says with the conviction of someone who's been playing the instrument all his life and looks a very healthy 73 years old.

While some songs in the sanshin repertory deal with happy themes, many reflect the often tragic history of the vanished Ryukyu kingdom, such as one that tells the story of how a woman and her family were forced by the government to move to Ishigaki from a neighboring island. She climbs the peak of Houra to get a glimpse of her former home, where her lover still lives. A stone on the summit is said to be shaped like a crying woman.

Tamayose sings the song, accompanying himself on the sanshin, his voice quavering with restrained passion. This must be what it's like when you're somewhere deep in the Mississippi Delta listening to the country blues at the source.

And like the blues, the music of Okinawa will likely continue to be a touchstone for Japanese musicians when they need a roots reference point.

文化的にも地理的にも沖縄は日本のディープ・サウスと呼べる。そのエキゾチックな音楽は、邦楽ではなくワールドミュージックの扱いを受けている事が多い。民謡との接点を失ってしまった本州とは違い、日本の中で唯一伝統音楽が現代文化を支える重要な役割を担っている地域。

この三線音楽の原形は今でも石垣島で耳にすることができる。熱帯特有ののんびりとした雰囲気の中イモクズアンダアギーをほおばりながら三線老師、タマヨセチョウダンの奏でる調べに身を委ねると、東京の喧騒が遥か遠い世界のようだ。「三線は心の傷を癒し、疲れから回復させる力がある」との73才の言葉には説得力がある。タマヨセの三線と静かなる情熱に震える歌声はミシシッピーのカントリーブルースに共通するものがある。多くの欧米のミュージシャンがブルースにルーツを見い出すように、沖縄音楽はこれからも日本人ミュージシャンの一つの拠り所として継承されていくだろう。

琉球音楽に欠かせない三線は中国から伝わり、本州では三味線へと形を変えた。琉球王国の崩壊の哀しい歴史を扱うものも少なくない。明るい曲も多いが、には

Okinawa is not exactly a hotbed of Latin music, but it does boast one excellent Latin band in the form of the Diamantes. The band is led by Japanese-Peruvian Alberto Shiroma, whose ancestors came from Japan's southernmost prefecture. Shiroma, who sings in both Spanish and Japanese, moved to Okinawa to "find his roots." In the process he put together the Diamantes, who recorded their debut album, Okinawa Latina, in 1993. Besides Shiroma's unique bicultural perspective, the band boasts an excellent Santana-esque guitarist in Tarbo, formerly with Okinawa hard-rock band Murasaki.

ペルー人アルベルト城間は自分のルーツを見つけるため沖縄に移住し、ディアマンテスを結成。城間の日本語・スペイン語による歌もさることながら、ハードロックバンド紫に在籍していたターボの、サンタナを彷彿とさせるギターも聴き逃せない。

Diamantes

57

Tokyo Bibimbap Club

伝統音楽に目を向ける一方で、上々颱風やザ・ブーム、坂本龍一のようにアジアにインスピレーションを受けるアーチストもいる。しかし日本とアジア音楽の純正ハイブリッドとなると難しい。政治的だったパック・ボーは抜けたものの、パワフルにそして豊かな声量で歌うピョン・インジャと日本でも有数のギターリスト春日博文による東京ビビンバクラブは韓国・日本・レゲエミュージックが自然な形で融合した希有なケースではないだろうか。

Besides drawing on homegrown musical traditions, Japanese pop sometimes looks to the rest of Asia for musical inspiration. Shang Shang Typhoon, for one, have made effective use of the Chinese *urhu* and its plaintive, violin-like sound, while the distinctive sound of the Indonesian *gamelan* pops up in the music of the Boom and Ryuichi Sakamoto, for example.

But full-fledged Japanese-Asian musical fusions are rare. An exception is Tokyo Bibimbap Club (TBC), a unique collaboration between veteran Japanese and Japanese-Korean musicians. Their eponymous 1996 debut album is an obscure classic.

Singer Pyeon Inja used to be Shang Shang Typhoon chanteuse Satoko Nishikawa's vocal teacher, and it's easy to see why Nishikawa — an amazing singer in her own right—would want to learn from Pyeon. Banging a *changoo* drum, cutting an exotic figure in her traditional Korean *chima chogori* dress, she sings in rich, powerful tones. No less impassioned are the mainly Japanese vocals of the band's other Japanese-Korean member, Pak Poe, who also plays guitar. The most overtly political member of TBC, Pak left the band in 1996 to devote all his energies to his own band, Kirikyogen.

"One part of me wants to express a Korean style in Japan. Our culture has its origins partly in Korea, although now it doesn't appear that way," says Pak. "I believe we're like a family, so why don't we become a little more familiar with Korean culture? Anyway, I enjoy playing Korean-style music. To me it's pure fun."

TBC's Hirofumi "Hachi" Kasuga is one of Japan's best guitarists—"I'd put him in the same category as Clapton," enthuses an American musician who's a close observer of the Japanese music scene. Formerly with legendary '70s band Carmen Maki and Oz, Kasuga, like many Japanese rock musicians of his generation, eventually grew dissatisfi with the music biz and instead of pursuing pop stardom, started explori the roots of Japanese music.

"I was playing Korean percussion instruments just for pleasure," explai Kasuga laconically. "I lived in Korea fo a year to study music. After coming ba to Japan, I wasn't interested in Weste popular music. I wanted to do someth different. I didn't imagine forming a ba like Bibimbap. Everything happened spontaneously."

The music of TBC is equally rootec in the Korean *boncha* beat and reggae since Pak Poe played in a reggae ban in San Francisco for ten years. Unlike gimmick bands like A'jyota, TBC's eclee fusion of Korean, Japanese, and regg music isn't forced and unnatural.

86年に親しい友人が集まり甲府に誕生したザ・ブームは翌年には東京でホコ天の常連となっていた。当初英系スカに影響されていたが、92年アルバム「思春期」によって日本の伝統音楽の一つである沖縄音楽と出会う。「島唄」のヒットによりJポップ界にその位置を築き、その後も様々な民族音楽を取り入れたアルバム作りを展開している。単なる借り物や真似事と批判するのではなく、彼等の飽くなき音楽への探究心を評価したい。

The Boom

The Boom was formed in 1986 by a group of friends from the city of Kofu, about 100 kilometers west of Tokyo. In 1987 they moved to the capital and soon became regulars on the hokoten street-band scene. They were first heavily influenced by the British ska movement, but by the time of their fourth album, 1992's *Shishunki*, they had discovered their own country's rich musical heritage, specifically the sounds of Okinawa. "Shima Uta" ("Island Song"), a track from that album, became a huge hit (with sales of 1.5 million copies), and the Boom were firmly established as being in the vanguard of the ethnic-pop movement.

Their 1994 album, *Faceless Man*, saw them add other ethnic colors to their sonic palette as they explored the gamelan music of Indonesia and collaborated with Singapore's Dick Lee.

On their 1994 album, *Kyokuto Samba* ("Far East Samba"), the Boom adopted a Latin musical persona. Miyazawa's smooth vocal style was well suited to the sensuous, sinuous sounds of the bossa nova and other Latin styles covered by the band. In 1994 Miyazawa tried his hand at reggae in a mini-album he did with singer Yami Bolo titled *Love Is Dangerous*.

In 1996 the Boom continued to draw on the rich Malaysian/Indonesian idiom on the stellar album *Tropicalism -0°*. What makes their music special is that their willingness to take musical risks. Some might accuse the Boom of plundering other musical traditions, but what comes through clearly regardless of the musical personae they adopt is a genuine sense of musical exploration, and not mere gimmickry.

Sandji

Sandji Sandji Sandji

地理的にはアジア大陸に近い日本も、こと文化に関して、特に言語は全く別の話である。日本語と北京語は英語とフィンランド語ほどかけ離れている。もちろんマレー語やインドネシア語との共通点は殆ど皆無。だからこそサンディーのように一枚のアルバムの中で北京・マレー・インドネシア・英各語で歌うアーティストは珍しい。ハワイ出身の彼女は70年代に故坂本九に後押しされデビュー。オーストラリア、マレーシアでも成功している。

Japan may be geographically close to continental Asia, but culturally—especially when it comes to language—it's a different story. Mandarin Chinese is as different from Japanese as English is from, say, Finnish. The same goes for Malay and Indonesian, two other Asian languages with next to nothing in common with Japanese.

So it's pretty unusual to find a Japanese performer singing in Mandarin, Malay, Indonesian as well as English—on the same album, no less.

But that's exactly what Sandii Suzuki did on her 1994 album, *Dream Catcher*. Sandii, as she is known professionally, recorded alternate-language versions of various tracks on *Dream Catcher* to increase its appeal in specific Southeast Asian markets. The album is an intriguing blend of Sandii's pop-oriented vocals and slick production liberally spiced with different Southeast Asian instruments and background vocals. It reflects Sandii's longstanding interest in the musical styles of the Asia-Pacific region, which she traces to having grown up in Hawaii.

After moving to Japan in the 1970s, Sandii made her professional debut with the support of people such as the late Kyu Sakamoto (who sang the only Japanese song ever to reach No. 1 on the Billboard singles chart, "Ue o Muite Aruko," known overseas as "Sukiyaki"), in 1963. Her first solo album, *Eatin' Pleasure*, came out in 1980 and was produced by the ubiquitous Haruomi Hosono.

Sandii then formed the band Sandii and the Sunsetz with Kubota, and achieved a fair degree of success outside Japan, touring Australia and Europe, as well as performing at Jamaica's Reggae Sunsplash. She released her second solo album, *Mercy*, which contained updated versions of classics such as "Sakura" and "Sukiyaki" in 1990.

Sandii's 1992 album, *Pacifica*, saw her draw on a wide variety of Asia-Pacific styles, and her 1993 indie release, *Airmata*, consisted of her very convincing versions of well-known Indonesian and Malay pop tunes in their original languages.

The group known as Kodo was formed in 1981 by a community of people who had come to Sado Island in the Sea of Japan ten years earlier to devote themselves to the study of the traditional "taiko" Japanese drum. They wanted not only to study and preserve traditional Japanese performing arts, but also to create new directions for what they believe are still vibrant art forms.

What makes Kodo special among Japanese traditional music enthusiasts is the emphasis they place on cultural exchange through joint performances, festivals and workshops. In 1981 Kodo began its continuous "One Earth Tour," Kodo's major vehicle for its performance activities. They've been just about everywhere on the planet, and as a result for many people, Japanese drumming is synonymous with Kodo.

Every summer Kodo sponsors a three-day percussion and arts festival called "Earth Celebration" which brings performers from all over the world to Sado Island.

Although best appreciated live, Kodo have released a number of albums, the latest of which, Ibuki, was produced by New York's legendary Bill Laswell, who gives Kodo's music a new ambient dimension.

和太鼓に引かれ佐渡に渡った人々が結成したのが鼓童。伝統芸能としての継承だけではなく、アートとしての新しい方向性を追及する為だ。鼓童が注目される理由は、その幅広いジョイント活動とワークショップ。81年からのONE EARTH TOURは彼等の活動の基盤であり、地球上の様々な場所で演奏している。ライブで堪能したいが伝説的ビル・ラズウェルのプロデュースによるアルバム「いぶき」では新しいアンビエントな側面が楽しめる。

Kodo

uya ブヤ

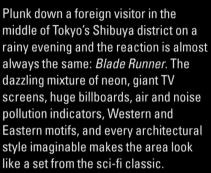

EPICENTER OF JAPANESE YOUTH CULTURE

Plunk down a foreign visitor in the middle of Tokyo's Shibuya district on a rainy evening and the reaction is almost always the same: *Blade Runner*. The dazzling mixture of neon, giant TV screens, huge billboards, air and noise pollution indicators, Western and Eastern motifs, and every architectural style imaginable makes the area look like a set from the sci-fi classic.

It's where Japan's music, fashion, and other pop trends are born and picked up by the media. It's home to what's billed as the world's biggest record store and a myriad of small outlets that make it one of the best places on the planet to buy music. It's crude, rude, flashy, and trashy.

In Japanese, Shibuya literally means "bitter valley," but it's where you'll find some of the sweetest sounds in Japan. Its "live houses" offer pop pickers a chance to catch tomorrow's superstars while they're still paying their dues, while its larger clubs and halls feature a rich array of established acts from Japan and around the world.

It's the epicenter of Japanese youth culture—the kind of place where if you're over 25, it feels like it's time to check into the old folks' home.

Homeless Heart

Kabocha Shokai

渋谷は世界でも有数のストリート・ミュージシャンが集まる街でもある。エレクトリック・シタールを弾く男やフルコスチュームのスコットランド・バグパイプ吹き、「コンドルは飛んでいく」を繰り返すアンデスバンドに、歌謡曲を歌うカフカフドゴシコやデュエット、ホームレス・ハート。しかし、渋谷で最も伝統的なストリートミュージシャンと言えばチンドン屋。時代に取り残されているかのようで、しっかりと街に溶け込んでいる。

Music on the Street

The streets of Shibuya provide a backdrop for some of the best street musicians in the world. A one-man bands jostles for space with an electric sitar player, a Scottish bagpipe player attired in full highland regalia belts out favorites, and a troupe of Peruvian musicians neatly decked out in traditional Andean garb play "El Condor Pasa" over and over until you wish the damned bird would fly away and be done with it. Local bands such as kayokyoku revivalists Kafu Kafu Dogo Shico and duo Homeless Heart perform "street lives" to promote their music. Late in the evening, a jazz trio sets up in a narrow street bounded by two large buildings, causing their licks to echo through the night.

Of course, many of Shibuya's street entertainers are fit for entertaining streets and not much else.

Shibuya's most traditional street musicians are the chindonya, colorfully made-up and attired characters, male and female, who are hired by new restaurants and other establishments to advertise their presence in the neighborhood. They do this by banging drums and cymbals and playing a clarinet in a jaunty style that is instantly recognizable as that of chindonya. They're a common sight in Shibuya, eccentric leftovers from another era who blend in with the area's benign chaos.

Kenji Ozawa

Kahimi Karie

これだけの音楽があふれる渋谷という街で　渋谷らしい音楽はいったいあるのだろうか？　答えは√es。一般的に渋谷系アーチストは、ミスチルのようなトップJポップバンドよりも洗練され、こだわりをもっているという。ピチカート・ファイブ、カヒミ・カリィ、小沢健二らがその代表。ホームレス・ハートを扱うエピック関係者によるとはっきりと決められているわけではないが、英米系ポップに似てフレキシブルで軽い感じだという。

The Shibuya Sound

With all this music coming out of Shibuya, is there in fact a distinct Shibuya sound?

"Yes, there is," says promotion company staffer Hisae Ariga emphatically. "It's more sophisticated and stylish than (leading pop-rock group) Mr. Children. *Shibuya-kei* (Shibuya-style) artists like Pizzicato Five, Kahimi Karie, and Kenji Ozawa care more about their sound than other pop musicians."

Epic/Sony A&R staffer Ken Kishi, who handles Homeless Heart, is more equivocal: "It's difficult to say, because there's no strict meaning of the term. It's a little bit different from other Japanese pop music—it's closer to the feeling of British or American pop. It's a flexible, light feeling."

P-5

60年代のポップカルチャーにシュールなひねりを加えたピチカート・ファイブは「渋谷系」の代表。映画オタク＆レコードコレクター小西康陽と元ポータブル・ロックのボーカル野宮真貴にとってはキッチュとかっこいいは同義語だ。2人はこのユニークで鋭い感性によって海外でもファンが増え続けている。まるで60年代フランスのスパイ映画から抜け出して来たかと思えば、レトロなSFに出てくる惑星のバーホステスのようなコスチュームを着てみたり、野宮は様々な60年代スタイルをクールな視線でとらえ自分の中で消化させる。音楽は折衷主義。ピチカートが影響を受けたとするアーティストはYMOやプラスチックスからBootsy Collins、60年代レトロ未来感覚、70年代ソウル、「ティファニーで朝食を」、果てはBeasty Boysまでなんでもアリなのである。米アトランティックレコード担当者は、ウォーホールが90年代にバンドを作ったらピチカートになるのではと評している。

PIZZICATO FIVE

More than other group, Pizzicato Five (P5) embodies the Shibuya-kei style, with its surreal spin on early to mid-'60s pop culture. To P5 members Yasuharu Konishi and Maki Nomiya, kitsch and hip are two sides of the same coin. This unique sensibility, which verges on out-and-out camp, has endeared the band to a growing number of cognoscenti overseas.

Record collector and film freak Konishi started Pizzicato Five in the mid-'80s, along with K-Taro Takanami, who later left the group. Nomiya, formerly of pop band Portable Rock, joined P5 in 1990. Her stock-in-trade is adopting various retro personae with a studied, ironic cool. Sometimes she looks like she's just stepped out of a 1960s French spy movie, other times she wears outrageous get-ups that suggest a hostess in some intergalactic cocktail lounge.

And, oh yes, the music...

"We don't like to limit ourselves to one type of music," says Konishi. No kidding: P5's publicity material lists the following as influences on the band: Yellow Magic Orchestra, Bootsy Collins, Juan Garcia Esquivel, 1960s retro-futurism, '70s soul music, *Breakfast at Tiffany's*, Brigitte Bardot,

Mendes, Van McCoy, the Five Americans, Burt Bacharach, the Japanese techno-pop group the Plastics, Steve Miller, Donovan, and the Bye Bye Birdie soundtrack. You get the idea: this is eclecticism with a capital E.

To some people, P5's music is all style and no substance, but to others their unique mixture of studied ironic cool and pop naiveté is hipper than hip. They're a studio band first and foremost—the kind of sonic pastiche in which Konishi specializes is not easily reproduced on stage.

P5 is also one of the few Japanese musical units to have had an impact overseas. Their 1994 American debut album, *Made in USA* (Matador Records), has sold more than 100,000 copies, while their second stateside release, 1995's *The Sound of Music by Pizzicato Five* (Matador/Atlantic) has sold more than 100,000 units.

"When I first saw them, it struck me that they're what Andy Warhol would have created if he were putting together a band for the '90s," Atlantic Records official Michael Krumper was quoted as saying in 1995. "Their use of videotape images during the show is really innovative, and they sample from every area of pop culture, reflecting their pervasive knowledge of pop music."

As you might expect from a group that puts so much emphasis on style, their overseas image-building efforts have been closely linked to the fashion world. The P5 track "Twiggy Twiggy/Twiggy vs. James Bond" was used in Robert Altman's 1994 look at the fashion world, *Pret a Porter* (aka *Ready to Wear*). And "Happy Sad," the first single from The Sound of Music by Pizzicato Five, was used on the soundtrack of the film *Unzipped*, the critically acclaimed documentary about New York fashion designer Isaac Mizrahi. The music video version of the single featured Nomiya hanging out with supermodels Naomi Campbell and Cindy Crawford.

COSA NOSTRA

ラテン、ロック、アシッドジャズ、R&B、ポップと様々なスタイルがブレンドされた渋谷系バンド、コーザ・ノストラの音楽には有無を言わさない魅力にあふれている。バンドの顔である女性ツインヴォーカルの一人鈴木桃子は帰国子女で、高校時代より英語で作詞をしてきたが、オリジナル・ラヴやコーネリアスを聞き、最近では日本語でもグループ感を出すことができると確信。日本語での作詞にも挑戦していきたいと意欲を見せている。

Cosa Nostra want to make you a musical offer you can't refuse. One of the most interesting acts identified with the Shibuya sound, Cosa Nostra are all over the map stylistically. Latin, rock, acid jazz, R&B, straight pop—these are just some of the band's musical reference points.

"We're often considered a Shibuya-kei group, and we don't mind it," says Cosa Nostra co-lead singer Momoko Suzuki, who worked at ad agency McCann Erickson before joining the group. "In fact, it can work to our advantage, because people might buy our albums if they like the Shibuya-kei sound." The band formed back in 1991 when producer Tetsutaro Sakurai began a project to put together recordings by Azabu-based DJs. About twenty DJs joined, including members of UFO and Tokyo Number One Soul Set. At that time, Cosa Nostra's sound was what Suzuki terms "underground," with an emphasis on instrumentals.

"About two years later, to sharpen the group's image and give it a wider appeal, we started to try playing more songs with words and fewer instrumental tracks," says Suzuki. The line-up stabilized with two DJs, one bassist, and two singers, Suzuki and Reiko Oda.

"The music we play is 'Cosa Nostra music'," says Oda, who was a model before joining the band. "Many of our songs are jazz-flavored, but we don't want to stick to just one style. We want to try whatever we want. But it's true the sound was kind of acid-jazz before the current line-up became fixed."

Suzuki and Oda sing in both English and Japanese. Suzuki, who spent much of her childhood overseas, writes the English lyrics. "I started to write lyrics when I was in high school," she says. "I wrote them in English, because it was easier and more natural for me.

"I don't feel any difference between singing in English and in Japanese," explains Suzuki. "Until recently, I used to think English could express the 'groove' of emotions or feelings better than Japanese. But I found I was wrong after listening to many groove-oriented Japanese songs by Original Love, El Malo, Cornelius, and the Escalators. It's all up to how well you write lyrics, and that's what I'll try from now on."

Notes Oda: "There are many new developments on the Tokyo club scene now. And so a lot of people who preferred foreign music and didn't pay attention to Japanese music are changing their minds. I think that's because the scene is much improved and more sophisticated compared to what it was ten years ago."

theatre brook

One of the best Shibuya-kei bands, Theatre Brook, is led by a guy from Osaka, Taiji Sato. But their sound is pure Shibuya: jazzy, clever, tight and way, way hipper than 99% of Japanese pop. Sato is a charismatic figure in the tradition of Shoukichi Kina, given to rambling lectures about life, the universe, and everything else in interviews. His conversation is full of references to positive vibrations, maintaining the balance between good and evil, and other neo-hippie thought.

Sato totally dominates Theatre Brook, playing amazingly articulate, funky guitar (a Les Paul is his instrument of choice) and singing with a passionate lyricism. The band's 1996 debut album *Talisman* is highly recommended.

His conversation is full of references to positive vibrations, maintaining the balance between good and evil, and other neo-hippie thought.

リーダー佐藤タイジは大阪出身でありながら、ジャジークレバーなシアター・ブルックは渋谷系そのもの。洗練度は群を抜いている。喜納昌吉に似た伝説のカリスマ性を持った佐藤様のインタビューは、いつも人生や世界観についての思想が語られ、彼のギタープレイ（ギターはレスポール）と情熱溢れる歌がバンドのサウンドそのものと言って過言ではない。96年にリリースされたデビューアルバム「タリスマン」は必聴。日本のポップ界でもそのその。

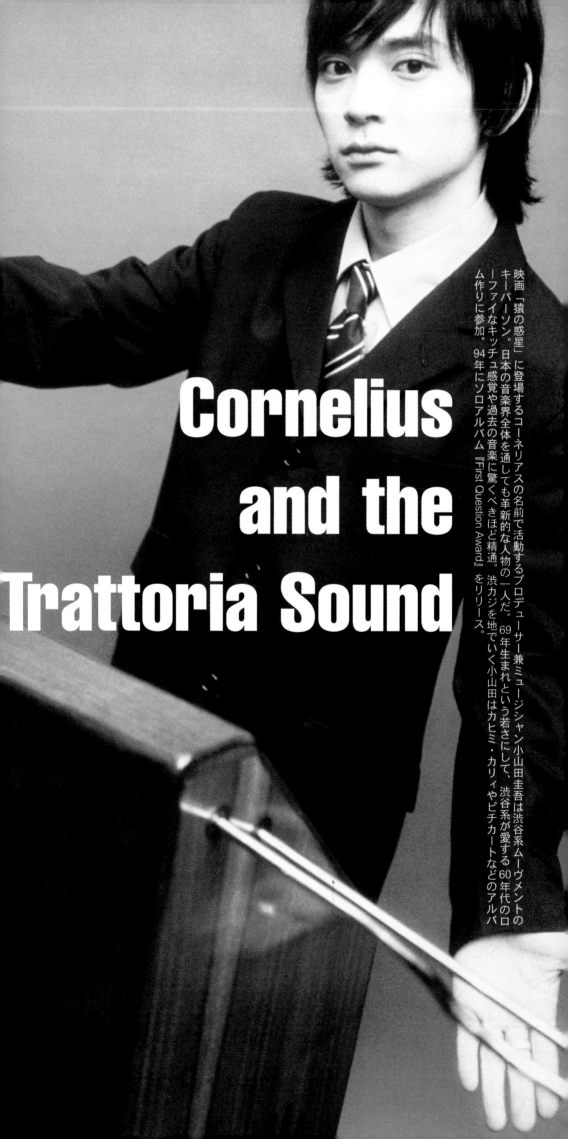

Cornelius and the Trattoria Sound

映画「猿の惑星」に登場するコーネリアスの名前で活動するプロデューサー兼ミュージシャン小山田圭吾は渋谷系ムーヴメントのキーパーソン。日本の音楽界全体を通しても革新的な人物の一人だ。69年生まれという若さにして、渋谷系が愛する60年代のロ—ファイなキッチュ感覚や過去の音楽に驚くべきほど精通。渋カジを地でいく小山田はカヒミ・カリィやピチカートなどのアルバム作りに参加。94年にソロアルバム『First Question Award』をリリース。

¥ 160,000

160,000 YEN FOR A PAIR OF LEVI'S

On the Shibuya fashion front, the never-ending quest to revive past trends has led to the current absurd situation in which secondhand "E" series Levi's jeans from the '60s fetch prices as high as ¥160,000 a pair at the boutiques in the section of Shibuya near the Harajuku fashion district.

Other stores and streetside stalls sell baggy pants, baseball caps, and T-shirts with the *de rigueur* marijuana-leaf emblem (a decidedly rebellious gesture in a country where pot-smoking is very much taboo).

End of the night

古いものをリバイバルさせ、デッドストック物を追い続ける渋谷ファッションの最先端、原宿に近いエリアのブティックでは60年代物リーバイスEシリーズが一本16万円で売られるという馬鹿げた状態になっている。また、路地に立ち並ぶ店先では、ダボパンや野球キャップと共に、「葉っぱ」がタブーとされている日本では反社会的とも取られかねないマリファナリーフのTシャツ等も売られている。

Late at midnight the streets of Shibuya are filled with the seismic rumblings emanating from "bass blasters" and trucks cruising the area and looking for action. Despite the somewhat menacing presence of the brass boys and other street "toughs," the vibe in Shibuya, as elsewhere in Japan, is usually peaceful. Fights are rare. Many kids hang out in Shibuya after midnight and just sit on the street, waiting for something to happen.

The Shibuya experience adds up to an amazingly diverse pop culture menu that offers spiritual sustenance for Japanese fed up with a society that often stifles individuality and creativity. Just what pop trends will next emerge from Shibuya's rich cultural cauldron is anybody's guess.

"Indie" is a loose, catch-all term that means different things to different people. In the Japanese context, it can mean bands and labels outside of the commercial mainstream represented by the Recording Industry Association of Japan's 29 member companies.

n d

It also describes an attitude, a sometimes bloody-minded refusal to compromise. For example, Super Junky Monkey, with its radical, over-the-top music, still has that crucial "indie" vibe, even though the band is signed to Sony Records.

There was a time when, in Japan, indie basically meant underground: deliberately obscure, often to the point of unlistenability. The prevailing ethos seemed to be the weirder, the better. But Japanese indies are now placing as much emphasis on listenability as lunacy, and the result is some of the best music around.

ies

様々な人の間で、様々な意味で使われる曖昧な言葉「インディーズ」。日本においては主にメジャー商業ベースの流れに乗っていないバンド、もしくは日本レコード協会加盟の29社以外のレーベルを指す。また、スーパー・ジャンキー・モンキーのようにソニーと契約していても、その妥協を許さない姿勢からインディーズと呼ばれる場合もある。一昔前はインディーズ即ちマイナーというイメージがあり、異様であればあるほど、難解であればあるほど良いとされていたが、最近では聴きやすさも加わって、今、最もクールなサウンドを作り出している。

In 1993 keyboardist/producer/scenemeister Hoppy Kamiyama realized that if the majors were going to ignore the explosion of musical talent taking place right under their noses, the only thing to do was to start an indie label.

Kamiyama called his label God Mountain ("kami" = god, "yama" = mountain). Its roster is uncompromisingly eclectic: there's the psychedelic funk of Optical 8, the sonic mishmash of Ground Zero (a joint project by guitarist Yoshihide Otomo, "scream sax savant" and Japanophile John Zorn, the Boredoms' Eye Yamatsuka and Australian drummer

Tony Buck) and the Pugs, which God Mountain's promo handout describes as "King Crimson covering Daisy Chainsaw."

One of Kamiyama's latest projects is a five-member group that until late 1996 played under the name Olivia*New*Ton*John.

"The name came to me suddenly one morning. I woke up and the name Olivia Newton-John was in my head. It doesn't have any meaning," says Kamiyama while consuming a curry at an Indian restaurant.

The band now goes under the name O*N*T*J, but the music is just as out-there as before.

With his red-dyed hair and retro-kitsch clothes, Kamiyama is not exactly Joe Salaryman. Seated behind the keyboards with O*N*T*J at Shibuya live house La Mama, he's unrecognizable in a tacky dress, green feather boa, blonde wig and thick pancake makeup. In his sober suit and slicked-back hair, tuba player Bon Juro looks like a particularly uptight accountant, while drummer Whacho's otherwise normal-looking face is dominated by a large painted-on *Salvador Dali* mustache. Guitarist Tesshi is the straight man of the group, who, like the others, is a bloody good player.

HOPPY KAM
AND GOD

メジャーレーベルが依然として多くの才能を無視し続ける中、キーボード奏者兼プロデューサー、ホッピー神山が自らアーティストを育てる為にレーベルを設立したのは93年。日本のインディーズとしては初めてヨーロッパ圏でのライセンスを獲得した彼の God Mountain（＝神山）レーベルが抱えるアーティストはバラエティに富ぶ。サイケ・ファンク系のオプティカル8や形容し難いグランド・ゼロに、キングクリムゾンがデイジーチェーンソーをカバーした」ような the Pugs 等。80年代のインディーズシーンは二つに分けることができたという。ブレイクを狙うわけでもなく、ひたすら自分達の音楽を求めるノイズ系・ハードコア系と、その他大方は、×Japanのようにメジャーを夢見るバンド。しかしそれもメジャーを夢見るバンド達も自分達の音楽を聴いてもらいたいと思うようになった。結果、インディーズファンが急増した。90年代に入り一転した。インディーズの音楽は明るく、聴きやすくなり、バンド達も自分達の音楽を聴いてもらいたいと思うようになった。結果、インディーズファン

singer HoneyHK's sensible clothes, healthy hairdo and seasoned, thick tattoo over ... do not necessarily ... the sound you'd associate with ... it's hard to imagine your annoying ... neighbors with ones like "Boojou" ... and ... number of ... Shibuya-Go? ... with an odd mix, sounds the ambiance that calls the cheesy sonic identity ... item that ... has only ... number of "N.G." ... whose first album was called echo 1988 on ... is a compelling ... it is much mutant ... natural as rock 'n' roll, think of lounge

music from a Holiday Inn somewhere out in the asteroid belt.

"Five years ago or so there were two types of indies music in Japan: some deep underground bands playing noise and hard-core, who didn't care about being popular. With the rest—about 90%—made up of bands that wanted to make it to the majors, such as X (now known as X Japan).

"But at the beginning of the '90s, there were a lot of changes," Kamiyama continues. "Deep underground wasn't 'deep' anymore—it became brighter and more accessible, and so the number of indies fans increased. Indies artists are more open-minded—they want their music to be heard. Indies music is more interesting now."

HoneyHK, this time in her pneumatic sex god-dess guise, fronts yet another Kamiyama project, the seven-piece band known as the Pugs. Their dense, driving music is structured enough to be access-ible, but definitely not for the faint of eardrum. Riffs pile up one after another in a relentless sonic assault that sometimes sounds like the Tubes and Yoko Ono on MDA. Their 1996 album, *Mushi Mushi Tengoku*, is an accomplished slice of brain-altering noise (in the best sense). The same year saw their U.S. debut on the Casual Tonalities label with the album *Pugs Bite the Red Knee*, comprising material from their Japanese releases.

YAMA MOUNTAIN

Olivia★New★Ton★John

The Indies Gospel

For true believers in the indies gospel, the majors are the bad guys.

Says "Geees" Kosugi of the Howling Bull indie label group: "The promotion people at the major labels only target the mass media, and bands signed to the majors try to sound 'average' so they can appeal to the mass audience. They all sound the same."

"People at major labels don't have the eyes and ears to find anything new," says Kazutoshi Chiba, president of Bad News Music Publishing Inc., which runs three indie labels and the Bad News music magazine. "Even if they do, because they're part of a corporation, they have to concentrate on the company's major artists."

The Japanese indies scene, in contrast, is characterized by an almost religious enthusiasm. Maybe that's because the people who run the labels actually like the music.

Chiba says Japanese indies are no longer merely farm teams for major labels.

"For many bands, there's no difference anymore between indies and the majors," he claims. "After a band makes a good record on an indie label, they may stay, they may not—there's not that much advantage anymore in being on a major label. This trend will accelerate."

Chiba claims Japanese music fans don't differentiate between majors and indies. "They're starting to listen to music according to their own taste—not what the media say," he claims.

In an attempt to get a piece of the action, some Japanese majors have started their own in-house indies-style labels.

Toshiba-EMI has its suite!supuesto! imprint, which features non-mainstream acts such as psychedelic revivalists HAL From Apollo '69, the Nelories, and Violent Onsen Geisha. And Japan's oldest record company, Nippon Columbia, has its Triad label, whose roster includes acts such as The Yellow Monkey and the Pugs.

That doesn't impress purists like Hiroshi Asada, who runs indies label group Seven Gods Music: "It's not that easy for the majors to pretend they understand indies style. The serious indies people know what they're doing."

Boryoku Onsen Geisha 暴力温泉芸者

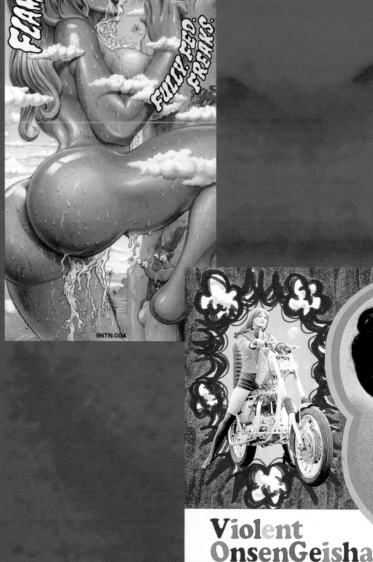

「メジャーのプロモ担当はマス・メディアを対象にし、契約したバンドに万人受けするサウンドを要求する」と、ハウリング・ブルの小杉。メジャーに対するインディーズの姿勢は世界共通。メジャー予備軍としての時代は終わり、流通が発達した日本のインディーズ界は今、勢いづいている。もうメジャーに移籍するメリットは少なくなっているからだ。この流れに乗り、メジャー会社も独自のインディーズレーベルを設立し始めている。

BNTN-004

Violent OnsenGeisha

QUE SERA, SERA (THINGS GO FROM BAD TO WORSE)

インディーズシーンでは女性が元気だ。特にベンテンレーベルだ。ヌードルズ等女性バンドばかりのレーベルだ。これらのバンドに共通するのは、プロの洗練された音と素人的な魅力の旨いバランス。特にフラメンコはメジャーでは敬遠されるセックスやドラッグに触れることが多かった。B級50年代路線を行く18号、今は解散してしまったがフラメンコ・ア・ゴーゴーやロリータ5678'sもカナダ、アメリカ等で精力的にツアーを行っている。

XXXXX XXX XXXXX XXX Where the Girls are

..., according to an old Japanese saying, are supposed to show deference to the male sex by walking three steps behind their man. But in the Japanese indies world, they're often way out in front of the menfolk. Being on the fringes of the Japanese music business means women—whether as artists, managers or label executives—have more freedom and creative scope then they generally do in the mainstream music biz.

Explains one key player in the Japanese indies scene, the Benten label's Shisaka Kimura:

"Female bands are more free," she states calmly. "They're less uptight about musical categories. For example, they'll do an 'unplugged' gig even if they're not really up to it, while a male hard-core band won't, because they're much more nervous about how they'll come across."

Not surprisingly, girl groups like the now-disbanded The Flamenco A Gogo, Pettey Booka, Lolita No. 18, and the Noodles dominate the Benten roster. Benten is also the Japanese licensee for New York female trash-rockers the Lunachicks.

To Kimura, it's simple: indie means good, major means... well, something else.

"There are so many great indies bands—at least they're great until they get involved with a major label," she claims. To Kimura's way of thinking, the Neiories and Shonen Knife lost their appeal when their musical skills improved and they signed with major labels.

Benten's acts straddle the line between amateur charm and professional slickness, although like indies bands everywhere, they still sometimes seem infatuated with the idea of dissonance and deliberate non-musicality.

Most Japanese pop acts avoid the slightest hint of controversy.

But many indies acts try to be as rebellious and outrageous as possible.

Few bands, for example, would take on Japan's No. 1 biggest record company by appearing on stage wearing T-shirts bearing the legend "Fuck Sony," which is exactly what The Flamenco A Gogo did at a CMJ Japan gig back in 1993. No doubt it was entirely coincidental that Super Junky Monkey and not the Flamencos were chosen as Japan's entry at that year's CMJ Music Marathon.

The Flamenco A Gogo's music was full of references to sex and drugs, which put them beyond the pale as far as Japanese majors are concerned. Song titles on The Flamenco A Gogo's 1994 album, *Fully Fed Freaks*, include gems like "Make Me Stinked," "Stoned Girls," and the immortal "Cool Baby Slut." Seiko Matsuda, eat your heart out.

Another spin on the girl-group dialectic comes in the firm of the 5678's, who with their tacky dresses and disheveled beehives look like B-girls from a sleazy '50s bar. And that's not meant to be a putdown. Their music recalls the Cramps, the legendarily bad Shaggs (gasp!) and pre-musical-competence Shonen Knife. They've toured the U.S., Canada, Australia and Europe, and have released an EP on U.S. indie imprint Sympathy for the Record Industry. Like Shonen Knife, you either love the 5678's, or you maintain an active dislike for them.

THE GREATEST ALL GIRL BANDS
IN THE WORLD!!!

Super Junky Monkey (SJM) is not your average Japanese girl group. Their music is an uncompromising blend of thrash, funk, hip-hop, and rock that's worlds away from the slick pap that dominates the Japanese charts.

A typical SJM show begins with a crashing guitar chord that would wake the dead, a relentlessly funky rhythm section and a tormented voice screaming lyrics like: "Spit on your past/ Spit on your brains/ Spit on your life/ Spit on yourself!"

This is definitely not Shonen Knife.

One of the most original bands to come out of Japan's exciting indies scene, Super Junky Monkey got started in 1991 when guitarist Keiko met vocalist Mutsumi Takahashi. Bassist Shinobu Kawai and drummer Matsudaaahh! joined later to complete the four-woman line-up. Musical influences cited by band members include Journey (!), King Crimson, Faith No More, James Brown, and Ozzy Osbourne. Keiko's hard-rock background shows in the killer riffs that are an SJM trademark.

拍手に恥ずかし気に答え、どこにでもいそうな女の子が4人、新宿リキッドルームのステージに上がった。また甘ったるいアイドルもどきバンドか？　と思った人はその炸裂するギターに、レベル計測不能のリズムセクションに、苦悩に満ちたシャウトに目を覚まされることだろう。それが日本のインディーズでも最もオリジナリティに溢れるバンドSuper Junky Monkey (SJM)だ。スラッシュメタル、ファンク、ヒップホップ、そしてロックが激しくぶつかり合うその音楽はヒットチャートを独占する洗練されたポップから

The Super Junky Monkey moniker has no special meaning– the band members say they just liked the sound.

One of the problems with Japanese indies bands is that while they're often great live, on CD they can be somewhat disappointing, especially when, as with the Boredoms, the visual/participatory side of the show plays a crucial role.

Super Junky Monkey, however, have been able to capture the energy of their live shows in their recorded work, starting with their first album, a live album titled *Cabbage*, released on indie label Riot in March 1994. One reason is their solid songwriting skills. Another is the band's willingness to experiment musically: not many Japanese bands make use of the Australian didgeridoo, which SJM did on a track titled "Love & Peace Hard Core" on their 1996 mini-album *Super Junky Alien*.

Super Junky Monkey were signed by Sony Records in 1994, but being on a major label hasn't tamed their sound–if anything, the band's music is getting more radically uncompromising.

The most striking thing about SJM is the sight of four small Japanese women laying down this sort of bone-crushing funk-metal.

"We don't think of our music as violent or anything, it's just natural—we play what we think is cool," says Takahashi. Unlike the monotone, one-dimensional music of many bands that go the noise/thrash route, SJM's songs are multi-layered, tightly played pieces that bear repeated listening. And despite SJM's generally mega-heavy style, the band also has a lighter feminine side. Take, for example, the schoolgirlish chants on their song "kioku-no-netsuzou" (which translates literally as "memory of fabrication").

All four SJM members collaborate on the music. Takahashi writes the lyrics, half the time in English, reflecting the band's long-standing desire to break out of their native Japan.

"We wanted to play in other places (outside Japan), any place," says the intensely serious Takahashi. "We weren't thinking of just the U.S. as a possibility, but it turned that it was in America that we first played overseas."

Her lyrics are mostly upbeat. "Open up your mind, open up your mind/ Think about it/ Heaven is now/ Heaven is now," Takahashi sings on "Buckin' the Bolts," but on another track from their *Screw Up* album, "Get Out," she delivers a blistering tirade:

You start movin' up and become such a snot
People you knew you stab in the back
Walkin' on heads then laugh as they crack.

SJM's first big break came in October 1993 when they won the CMJ Japan Battle of the Bands contest, which landed them a spot at the CMJ Music Marathon in New York the next month. Since then they've toured the U.S. regularly, building up a solid core of stateside fans.

The last word goes to Takahashi:

"If you're the kind of person
Who can't do anything on your own accord
Who feeds on the kindness of others
Who can't find happiness without exploiting
The weakness of those around you
I can only say
FUCK THAT NOISE."

(from "Fuck That Noise," on A-I-E-T-O-H)

遥か遠い。彼女達自身は、単にクールだと思う音楽を作っているだけで特にそれが激しいとは思っていないと事も無げに言う。アメリカですでに演奏した彼女達は常に日本の外でも活動したいと考え、歌は英語と日本語が半々。影響を受けたアーティストとしてジャーニー（！）、キングクリムゾン、フェイスノーモア、ジェームス・ブラウン、オジー・オズボーン等を上げている。ギタリスト、ケイコのハードロック指向がSJMのトレードマークである熱いギターリフに表われている。

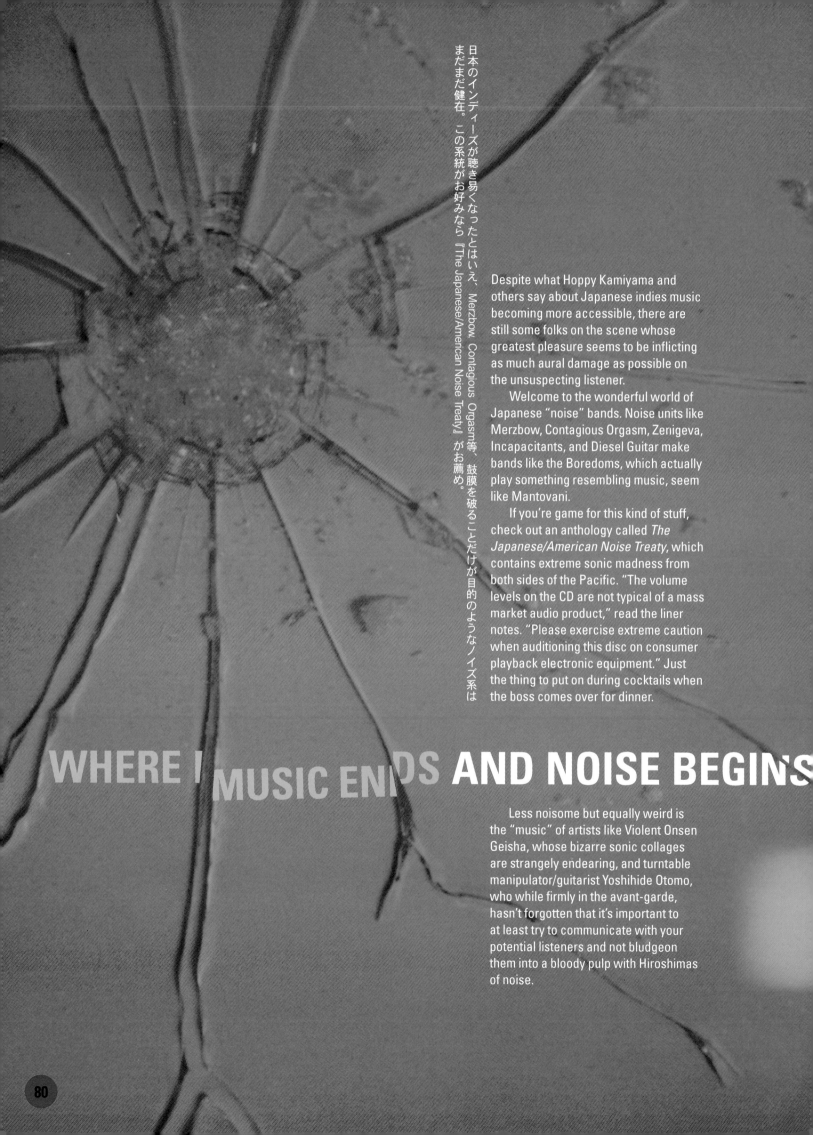

日本のインディーズが聴き易くなったとはいえ、Merzbow Contagious Orgasm等、鼓膜を破ることだけが目的のようなノイズ系はまだまだ健在。この系統がお好みなら『The Japanese/American Noise Treaty』がお薦め。

Despite what Hoppy Kamiyama and others say about Japanese indies music becoming more accessible, there are still some folks on the scene whose greatest pleasure seems to be inflicting as much aural damage as possible on the unsuspecting listener.

Welcome to the wonderful world of Japanese "noise" bands. Noise units like Merzbow, Contagious Orgasm, Zenigeva, Incapacitants, and Diesel Guitar make bands like the Boredoms, which actually play something resembling music, seem like Mantovani.

If you're game for this kind of stuff, check out an anthology called *The Japanese/American Noise Treaty*, which contains extreme sonic madness from both sides of the Pacific. "The volume levels on the CD are not typical of a mass market audio product," read the liner notes. "Please exercise extreme caution when auditioning this disc on consumer playback electronic equipment." Just the thing to put on during cocktails when the boss comes over for dinner.

WHERE MUSIC ENDS AND NOISE BEGINS

Less noisome but equally weird is the "music" of artists like Violent Onsen Geisha, whose bizarre sonic collages are strangely endearing, and turntable manipulator/guitarist Yoshihide Otomo, who while firmly in the avant-garde, hasn't forgotten that it's important to at least try to communicate with your potential listeners and not bludgeon them into a bloody pulp with Hiroshimas of noise.

FRICTION

Real veterans of the indies scene, Friction have been around since founding members Reck and Chiko Hige (who played in late-'70s New York "No Wave" bands Teenage Jesus and the Jerks and James Chance and the Contortions, respectively) returned to Japan in 1978 and started the band with guitarist Lapis. The band has existed intermittently since then. Bassist Reck occasionally tours and records with avant-jazz trumpeter Toshinori Kondo. They released an excellent comeback album titled *Zone Tripper* in 1995. This is dark, hard, stripped-down power-trio rock.

可愛いパンダの歌を歌いながら、観客の一人を相手にフェイクオーラルセックスを敢行する女性ヴォーカルはそういない。元吉本タレント、スプーンパームの本田みずほぐらいしか。ピチカートをアメリカに紹介した Matador Records が目をつけたのは、ジョニー・サンダースとリンク・レイが出会ったようだと評されるギターウルフ。78年以来のインディーズのベテラン、フリクションも 95 年には『Zone Tripper』で見事なカムバックを果たし頑張っている。

SPOONPERM

Not too many Japanese female vocalists perform mock oral sex on stage with a member (cheap pun intended) of the audience while also singing about how cute pandas are. In fact, only one springs immediately to mind: Spoonperm lead singer Mizuho Honda, who is one of the most original talents on the Japanese indies scene. The band's 1996 debut album, *Best*, is pure punk, with a large dose of social satire. The track "Panda" ruthlessly skewers the whole Japanese obsession with cuteness, as Honda shows off her amazing vocal skills, switching from a piercing screech to a guttural growl in the twinkling of an eye.

At one point Honda was on the fast track to Japanese media superstardom. Signed as a tarento to production agency Yoshimoto Kogyo, she was slated to be the latest female co-host of popular midday TV show "Waratte Iitomo," but a long period of illness put her career on hold. When Honda recovered, she found that she'd been left by the wayside, and so had to re-establish her showbiz connections on her own. That just might explain the anger in her singing.

GUITAR WOLF

Another Japanese hardcore outfit who've gained fans in the U.S., this three-piece band's guitarist, Seiji, is known for striking classic guitar-hero poses while playing very much out of tune. This hasn't prevented them from landing a record deal in the U.S. with Matador Records, the same people who introduced Pizzicato Five to an unsuspecting American public.

Their music can be described as Johnny Thunders meets Link Wray.

Like many Japanese indies operations, Bloody Dolphins started out by publishing a magazine (*Beikoku Ongaku*, or *American Music*), which features Japanese and foreign indies artists. Former rock journalist Daisuke Kawasaki runs Bloody Dolphins and the Cardinal label out of his house in a western Tokyo suburb—with the help of a staff of three.

"When we started publishing *Beikoku Ongaku* [in 1993], we'd always include a sampler CD of tracks by artists we'd featured in the magazine," says Kawasaki. "Then I realized I should just put out the CDs like other labels, so I started Cardinal Records."

One of Cardinal's coolest acts is Buffalo Daughter, a three-member group whose music ranges from straight-ahead rock to pop parody, with large chunks of Moog synthesizer thrown in for good measure.

BD members Sugar Yoshinaga (guitar, TB303, and vocal) and Yumiko Ohno (bass, analog synthesizer, and vocal), who played in four-woman band Havanna Exotica from 1987 to 1993, formed BD in 1993 with graphic designer Moog Yamamoto (turntables and vocals) and Chika Ogawa (drums and vocals).

The band debuted in 1994 with the mini-album *Shaggy Head Dressers*. Evidence of Buffalo Daughter's warped sensibility included a crazed, fast-paced track called "Health or Die," subtitled "For Karen Carpenter," and the minimalist mutant surf music of "Cold Summer." Despite such weirdness, Buffalo Daughter were asked to do the background music for a Listerine mouthwash commercial.

BD are one of a growing number of Japanese bands to develop a following overseas. They toured the United States in March 1996 and released a compilation album, *Captain Vapour Athletes*, on the Beastie Boys' Grand Royal label.

BLOODY DOLPHINS & BUFFALO DAUGHTER

スタッフ3名と西東京郊外の自宅でBloody Dolphinsとカーディナル・レコードを動かしているのは、元「ロッキングオン」ライター川崎大助。雑誌「米国音楽」出版に始まった活動はレコードレーベルへと発展、中でもBuffalo Daughterは特筆に値するバンド。不協和音を奏でながらも何故か滑らかなシンセをふんだんに取り込んだサウンドで、96年にはビースティボーイズのレーベルGrand Royalからアメリカデビューを果たしている。

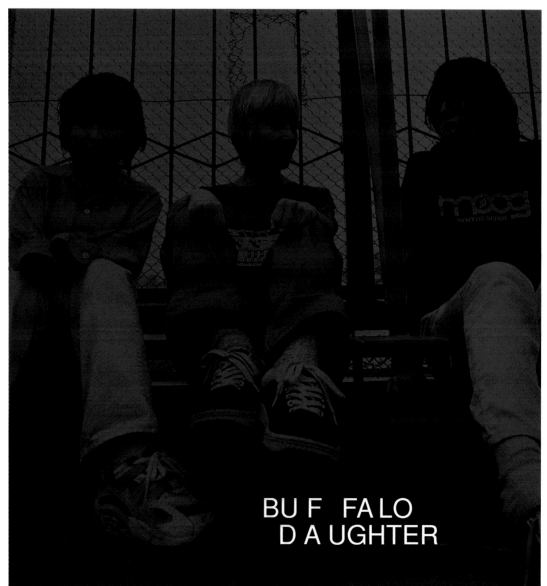

BUFFALO
DAUGHTER

Drugs and Censorship

日本の音楽界はドラッグに対して相当神経を尖らせている。93年には少年ナイフが『Catnip Dream』という曲で「葉っぱ」という表現がマリファナを想像させると、MCAビクターからクレームをつけられた。同年、テクノバンド、オーディオ・アクティブは『Free the Marijuana』をリリース、数年前、忌野清志郎はタイマーズ（大麻）を結成。我々には小さな事に思えるが、1グラムの大麻所持で逮捕された長渕剛を思えば大胆な行動といえる。

Drugs—the illegal kind—are a touchy subject in the Japanese music world. A good example of how sensitive Japanese record companies can be when there's the slightest hint of drug-related naughtiness came in 1993 when Shonen Knife (!) was asked by its record label, MCA Victor, to remove an alleged drug reference from a song on its album *Rock Animals*. The song, "Catnip Dream," originally included the line "Tane o maetara happa ga dettekita," which translates as "I sowed a seed in the ground and leaves came out." In colloquial Japanese, *happa* (literally, "leaves") means marijuana.

"The problem wasn't specifically the use of the word *happa*," said a label official. "The problem was one of general nuance."

"Catnip Dream" describes how catnip makes cats feel dreamy, and contains lines such as "Catnip wa nekko-chan no drug" ("Catnip is a kitty-kat drug"), which was not cut from the song.

Bass player Michie Nakatani, who wrote the song, says she was surprised when MCA Victor asked her to cut the "happa" reference. "I didn't mean it as a drug reference," she said. "I meant it as something a cat takes and enjoys, like medicine. But Japanese people are too

strict—they don't understand jokes. There are bands that say a lot worse things than us."

The English-language version of the song, which was featured in the overseas release of *Rock Animals*, contained the line: "Catnip is a kitty-kat drug/One puff, two puffs, high in a dream."

Techno/dub group Audio Active made a much less ambiguous statement about the demon weed with their 1993 track "Free the Marijuana," which was released uncensored, while veteran rocker Kiyoshiro Imawano tweaked his nose at the authorities some years back when he gave the name "The Timers" to a group he started up (*taima* is yet another Japanese slang term for marijuana).

This all may seem like pretty trivial stuff, but in a country where being found in possession of even the tiniest amount of dope can mean a quick trip to the slammer, they amount to brave gestures. In 1995 veteran artist Tsuyoshi Nagabuchi had a narrow escape when after being arrested for possession of one gram of marijuana, he was released from police custody after the men in blue determined the amount of the drug involved was "not sufficient to pursue the case."

DANCE MUSIC: AVEX + KOMURO

It wasn't too long ago that when it came to dance music, most Japanese record labels didn't know the difference between trance and the macarena. That was before indie label Avex and producer Tetsuya Komuro entered the picture and blew apart the complacent Japanese music scene by making dance music one of the biggest success stories in the Japanese music biz in the 1990s. Other labels have since gotten off their butts and moved onto the dance floor, but in Japan, dance music is still virtually synonymous with Avex.

From its humble beginnings in 1988 as a dance-music importer, Avex by the mid-'90s had become one of Japan's top five record companies. Its first taste of success came with astute marketing of overseas dance music, most notably through the "Juliana's" CD series, and by developing dance/pop acts such as trf, globe, and Namie Amuro into a new generation of Japanese pop megastars.

何がトランスでマカレナなのか。そんな区別さえつかなかったのもそんなに昔の話ではない。しかし、インディーズレーベルAvexとプロデューサー小室哲哉の登場により状況は一変。ダンス系は90年代最大の音楽ビジネスとなり、ダンスミュージック＝Avexという図式ができ上がっている。88年にダンス系音楽の輸入を細々と始めたAvexは、鋭いマーケティングとJuliana'sシリーズで、90年代半ばには国内5本の指に入るレコード会社へと成長した。

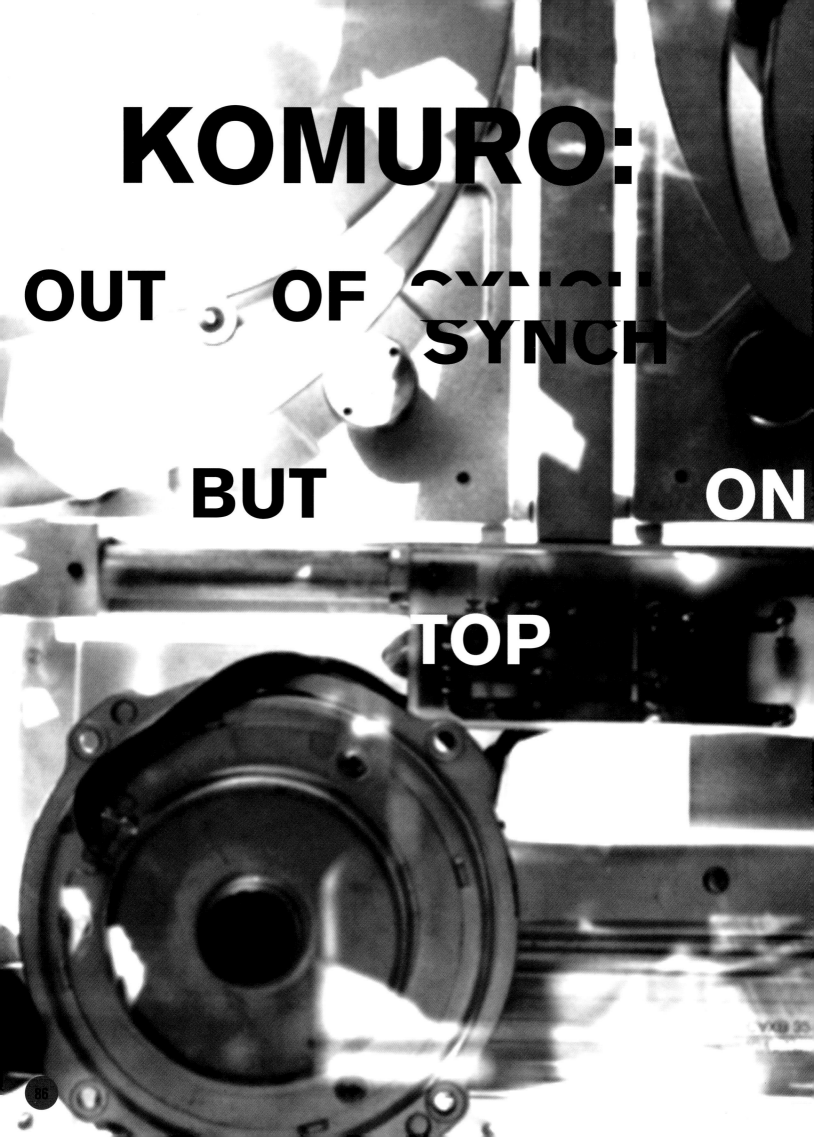

KOMURO:

OUT OF SYNCH SYNCH BUT ON TOP

90年代音楽シーンを独占する男・小室哲哉も多くの日本人と同様に仕事の虫だが、同時に一般人の生活とは少しずれているかもしれない。彼の典型的な一日は午後遅くのインタビューに始まり、制作ミーティング、そしてレコーディング、作詞・作曲と続き、自宅で朝までトラッキング、やっと眠りにつく。クラブ等には殆ど出かけないが、行っても楽しむどころか逆に新しい音楽を作らなければと言うプレッシャーを感じるという。

90年代始めまでプロデューサーは制作スタッフの一員として表に出ることはなかった。しかし、小室のレコード会社を超えたフリーとしての活躍が状況を変え、小林武史ら自分の音楽を追及する新しいタイプのプロデューサーが表われるようになった。アーティストがレコード

The man whose music dominates mid-'90s Japan leads a lifestyle that's quintessentially Japanese in its dedication to work—but at the same time just a bit out of sync with the rest of society.

"I'm a vampire," says Komuro, sitting in his sparsely furnished penthouse overlooking Tokyo Bay. "I often start off with an interview like this (the interview began at 5 P.M.), then attend a promotional meeting or a creative meeting, then I work on recording, composing, or writing lyrics.

"I do tracking here in my home until the morning, and then I go to bed. I don't go to night clubs so often… but when I do go to clubs, I can't relax or enjoy myself, because when I hear the music in the club, whether it's good or bad, I feel as if I have to go home and make new club sounds to pass on to club DJs who'd play them! When I'm in a place like Harajuku or Shibuya, among the crowds, I think, 'What kind of music would fit here and now?'"

Until the early '90s, Japanese record producers were usually faceless record label staffers. But Komuro's amazing track record, churning out hit after hit on a freelance basis for artists such as Yuki Uchida (King Records), Arisa Mizuki (Nippon Columbia), Ryoko Shinohara (Sony Records), Tomomi Kihala (on his own Orumok label), besides Avex acts such as trf, H Jungle With T, Namie Amuro, and globe, has cleared the way for other independent producers, such as Takeshi Kobayashi, to develop and promote their own individual sounds.

Total sales for albums and singles Komuro has produced since going independent are in the neighborhood of 100 million.

Komuro hesitates when asked whether he has his own sound: "When I make music, I don't try to make a sound that people can recognize as mine. But I guess it seems like the 'Komuro sound' anyway."

For someone who's doing rather nicely within the context of the Japanese record industry (his estimated annual income is between 3 billion and 4 billion yen), Komuro is surprisingly critical of the music biz.

"In America, artists and their managers have the right to promote their music to labels, distributors, promoters, and publishers. But in Japan, the record company decides almost everything.

They set up everything for the artist, even the producer, whom the artist has never met before. I don't think that's right.

"The artist should come first. I always say so in interviews like this, in the hope that the Japanese music production system will change. Otherwise Japanese artists will end up almost like company employees.

"Another problem is studio costs. Again, it's the record companies that have the money to pay the studio fees. If artists had to pay, they'd work more efficiently, I think."

Despite such criticism, Komuro is optimistic about the future of the Japanese music scene.

"In America, even 'idols' like Kris Kross are making rap music. Michael Jackson and Janet Jackson are idols. It's the same in Japan: 'idols' will be always be on the scene, but from now

on, they'll have to be 'quality' idols.

"I also think that in Japan music will be something more personal and individual, especially in Tokyo, where you have the largest variety of music and information in the world. So the Japanese music scene is going to become more chaotic than any other place. Ten years ago, I'd say it was New York, where there is a mixture of many different cultures. Now it's Tokyo. There may not be such a large number of nationalities living here, but the amount of information and data you can get in Tokyo is the largest in the world."

87

TRF

THE FIRST REQUIREMENT OF ANY DECENT POP SINGL
THEIR KEY PHRASES STICK IN YOUR HEAD
LIKE SO MUCH SONIC EPOXY

trf is an unlikely blend of talents. Lead vocalist is the cute-but-not-too-sexy Yuki, who shares the stage with female dancers Etsu and Chiharu and male dancer Sam, all of whom are in ridiculously good shape. Hovering in the background is DJ Koo, who mans the turntables while adding his own rap-style vocals from time to time. trf has led the way among the new wave of million-selling Japanese megaacts, selling just over 22 million albums and singles since their debut in 1993.

trf tunes like their first single, "EZ Do Dance," and "Boy Meets Girl" meet the first requirement of any decent pop single: their key phrases stick in your

Typically, Komuro writes all the words and music for trf releases, as well as taking care of synthesizer programming, "manipulation," and performance.

One recent trf single, "Love and Peace Forever," was a bit unusual for the group. Instead of the standard "boy meets girl" stuff, the song dealt with weighty issues such as world peace:

I've been waiting a long time for
the peace bell to sound out
I've been waiting a long time for
the dream

trfはユニークなタレントの集まりだ。キュートながらもユニセックスなボーカルのYuki、磨き抜かれた肉体を持つダンサーのEtsu、Chiharu、Sam。DJ Kooはバックでターンテーブルを回し、ラップスタイルのヴォーカルで参加することもある。93年のデビューから96年末までたて続けにメガヒットを出す活躍を見せた。特徴は『Boy Meets Girl』に代表されるキャッチーなメロディとテクノなリズムを華やかなミックスでまとめた小室サウンドである。

head like so much sonic epoxy. "EZ Do Dance" set the style for subsequent trf releases: a sprightly vocal by singer Yuki, a catchy chorus, and a techno-style rhythm track, all combined in a glossy, busy mix that's instantly identifiable as the Komuro sound.

Just how long the current trf line-up will remain intact is unclear, since the act is very much Komuro's creation. It may be that he doesn't want to tamper with a winning formula.

NAMIE AMURO

Komuro's most successful protégée is Okinawan Namie Amuro, who in the mid-'90s became what could be called Japan's first dance/pop idol. Japanese girls love her tough-but-sexy image, which they call the "amura" look. Even though she recently got pregnant, got married, and cut her hair (in that order) you can still take a walk around Tokyo's Shibuya district and see many, many girls with long henna-tinted hair decked out in the miniskirts and high platform shoes that, until recently, typified the amura style. Her debut album, *Sweet 19 Blues* (Avex Trax), has sold more than 4 million copies since its July 22, 1996 release.

Komuro's production work for Amuro is more R&B- and less pop-oriented, with guest artists such as Latin percussionist Sheila E. giving cuts on *Sweet 19 Blues* more of a funky edge than most Japanese recordings. Amuro has the baby face of an idol, but she's much more overtly sexual than past idol singers. Her voice is also surprisingly gutsy, and she's not a bad dancer either.

She professes to be as amazed by her unbelievably rapid rise to the top of the Japanese pop pantheon as anybody else. "It still hasn't hit me that the 'amura' phenomenon is really about me," she was recently quoted as saying. The final word on the amura phenomenon is not yet written. In defiance of the usual fate a Japanese woman faces (become a mom, kiss your career goodbye), Amuro recently announced that she plans to take a year off after her baby is born and then resume her career. An awful lot of her fans are watching anxiously, hoping she'll succeed.

Amuro is a graduate of the Okinawa Actor's School (OAS), which by the mid-'90s had become one of Japan's main sources of fresh dance/pop talent. The school gets 30 applications a day from Amuro wannabes. Amuro's four-girl backing group, the Super Monkey's [sic], attended the same talent academy, and in 1996 they established themselves as an independent act using the moniker Max. Yet another female quartet to come out of OAS is Speed, who made their professional debut in 1996 when their average age was just 13.5.

MAX

小室が手懸けた数多いアーティストの中で最も成功しているのか沖縄出身の安室奈美恵。90年代中期に日本で初めてのダンス／ポップアイドルとして人気を得た。彼女のベビーフェイスとは裏腹のタフでセクシーなイメージが女の子の憧れの的となり茶髪にミニスカート、上げ底靴のアムラーが後を絶たない。安室のサウンドはポップと言うよりはR&B系。彼女を生み出した沖縄アクターズスクールからはMAXやSPEEDもデビューしている。

VELFARRE

Avexは94年にディスコ経営へと乗り出した。日本ではディスコ市場は比較的小さく、しかもレコード会社経営よりもさらにリスクが大きいと言われたが、Avex会長の依田を思い止まらせることはなかった。三十億円をつぎ込みヴェルファーレを六本木にオープンすると発表した際、彼はナイトクラブ業界の努力が足りないことに触れ、エンターテイメント性や立地条件を向上させる必要があると述べた。ヰの成功によって、建てられたと言っても過言ではないバブリーにきらびやかなこのディスコは94年12月に開業。日本広しといえど、お茶室まであるディスコはヴェルファーレ以外にはないだろう。この間にもAvexはhitomiやm.c.A.Tなど次々とダンス系ミュージシャンをデビューさせ、この年、印税トップ3曲(『Wow War Tonight』・『Crazy Gonna Crazy』・『Overnight Sensation』)全てが小室によるという異例の状態。本人が実際に参加したglobeも同年デビュー、ファーストアルバムは日本初四百万枚の売上げを記録した。

In 1994, Avex decided to go into the disco business for itself. That raised a few eyebrows in the music business in Japan, since running a record label and running a disco require very different sets of skills. If the music business tends to be unstable, the disco/nightclub field is a veritable minefield which the unprepared enter at their own risk.

Avex Chairman Tom Yoda was undeterred. "Only a relatively few people go to discos in Japan," he said in announcing the 3-billion yen Velfarre project in Tokyo's Roppongi district. "The industry hasn't done enough to attract more customers. One reason is the lack of an entertainment infrastructure that is both well located and has an attractive environment."

Velfarre, which could be called the house that trf built, opened its doors to the public in December 1994. It's a glitzy, look-at-me kind of place decorated in what could be termed "early bubble economy."

It's probably the only disco in Tokyo, or anywhere, for that matter, that has a tea-ceremony room.

"I thought this would be a very good mix of Japanese classical culture and Western music such as techno and house," says Yoda. The idea is to provide a bit of Zen calm in the midst of Roppongi's hyper-charged atmosphere.

Meanwhile, Avex kept introducing new acts, such as rapper m.c. A.T. and idol-type singer Hitomi, a Komuro protégée, to cope with the Japanese music-buying public's apparently insatiable demand for dance music.

Komuro teamed up with comedian Masatoshi Hamada, aka "Hama-chan," in a unit called H Jungle With T, and scored a huge hit with the track "Wow War Tonight" which varied the Komuro formula a bit by using the rhythms of jungle-style dance music.

At one point in spring 1996 Komuro productions occupied five of the top songs on the Japanese hit singles chart — a feat no other Japanese record producer has ever achieved. He also wrote or co-wrote all five songs, which were:

1. "Don't wanna cry," by Namie Amuro (Avex).

2. "I'm Proud," by Tomomi Kahala (Orumok).

3. "FREEDOM," by globe (Avex).

4. "Love and Peace Forever," by trf (Avex).

5. "Baby baby baby," by dos (Orumok).

All five singles were "tie-ups" used as themes for TV dramas or commercials.

That unprecedented feat coincided with an announcement by Japanese music copyright society JASRAC that the top three songs in terms of copyright royalties collected (i.e., from record sales, karaoke performances, etc.) in the fiscal year ending March, 31, 1996, were all Komuro compositions—the first time one songwriter had ever done this. The songs were "Wow War Tonight," "Crazy Gonna Crazy," performed by trf, and "Overnight Sensation," also performed by trf.

The three-person globe unit is unusual in that Komuro is actually a member, instead of being simply the behind-the-scenes songwriter and knob-twirler. The other two members are singer Keiko and Marc Panther, a French MTV Japan presenter who raps in English. The group's eponymous 1996 debut made history when it became the first Japanese album to break the 4-million sales mark.

GLOBE

Japanese rap? Makes as much sense as Polynesian polkas, right?

Wrong. Rap and hip-hop are now as much a part of Japanese youth culture as McDonald's and Nike shoes. They've been adapted to suit domestic tastes in the same way rock, reggae, dance and other musical imports have successfully taken root in Japan.

Rap has had a big influence on Japanese youth culture, at least visually. The baggy pants, backward baseball caps/and the other attendant clichés of the homeboy look have become part of the fashion vernacular, although the automatic weapons and crack cocaine— thankfully—are missing. The attitude is

RAP HIP

there, though. The idea is to look as "gangsta" as possible, as if they were in South Central L.A. instead of Shibuya.

And the rap idiom itself suits the Japanese language, with its emphasis on word play.

In the early '90s rap was pretty well confined to the underground scene in Japan. Major record labels didn't know how to market overseas rap acts—even comparatively mainstream acts such as M.C. Hammer were just too far out in left field for them.

So it was left to indie labels like Tokyo's File Records and pioneering homegrown acts like Zingi, Scha Dara Parr, and VibraStone to spread the rap gospel. One of the most crucial sources of Japanese rap/hip-hop sounds in the early '90s was the Major Force label, which was distributed by File. Five producers/artists made up Major Force: Kan Takagi (who later went on to become a major rap act on his own), Masayuki Kudo, Toshio Nakanishi (formerly of the Plastics and Melon), Hiroshi Fujiwara and Yashiki Gota (formerly drummer with Mute Beat and Simply Red, now a freelance producer and leader of the band Gota and the Low Dog).

日本語ラップ？ポリネシアンなポルカぐらい違和感があると思うのは間違い。若者の間でラップ／ヒップホップはマクドナルドやナイキに負けない浸透ぶりだ。ロック、レゲエ、ダンス等海外からの音楽がみなそうであったように、ラップもまた日本流にアレンジされ、採り入れられた。ルーズパンツ、野球キャップ等の典型的なスタイルは、今やストリートファッションとして定着（ピストルやクラックなどが同時に輸入されなかった事は喜ぶべきだろう）。言葉遊び的な音楽性も日本語に合っているといえる。90年初期までは一部ファンのみに受け入れられていた。メジャーレコード会社が無視する中、インディーズからN=g、スチャダラパー、ビブラストーンといった純正グループが生まれた。この時期、大きな役割を果たしたのが高木完、屋敷豪太（元シンプリー・レッドのドラマー）等、5人のプロデューサー・アーティストで結成されたファイルのメジャーフォースレーベルである。

One wacky footnote in the evolution of Japanese rap was a 1991 album called *The Asian Rapper*, by Captain George Kayto, a Tokyo-based DJ with a Green Hornet complex. Kayto's attempts to rap in English ("If you ever have a chance to come to Asia/Visit Tokyo I am sure it will amaze ya!") somehow failed to connect with Japanese music fans, however, although the Captain deserved full credit for imagination: one track, "Dance to It," was a totally surreal blend of the killer riff from Led Zeppelin's version of "I Can't Quit You Baby" with the sounds of Awa Odori, a festival dance from the island of Shikoku.

ネ・ヨ・ダ
な・や・そ
ね・じゃ・ほ
い・た・そ
い・が・だ
ね

EAST END  YURI

Rap broke into the Japanese pop mainstream in 1994 with File's release of the single "Da Yo Ne" by East End X (pronounced "plus") Yuri. "Da Yo Ne" (which translates loosely as "that's the way it is") was the antithesis of hard-core hip-hop: vocalist Yuri, formerly of the all-girl Tokyo Performance Doll idol ensemble, backed by two-man unit East End, delivered a chirpy rap about boy-girl problems instead of the usual hip-hop rant about guns, 'hos, and other similarly charming subjects.

File was on to a winning formula: the *Da Yo Ne* mini-album sold close to 300,000 copies—unprecedented for a Japanese rap release. The project had actually originated with the Epic/Sony label, and so that label then took over the releases from File. With Epic/Sony's full marketing power behind it, "Da Yo Ne" soon topped the one-million sales mark. Its success inspired Epic/Sony to release several alternate versions of the single in regional Japanese dialects, such as "So Ya Na" by Osaka's West End X Yuki (*so ya na* is the Osaka dialect's equivalent of *da yo ne*). In Hiroshima, it became "Ho Ja Ne," and in Sendai, "Da Cha Ne." Until "Da Yo Ne," Japanese rap artists had mostly done Japanese versions of American rap songs. But because of the difference between American and Japanese societies, Japanese kids couldn't relate to the American style, says an Epic/Sony staffer. The lyrics of "Da Yo Ne" resemble a conversation among Japanese teens, thus making it easier to relate to.

『DA・YO・NE』のヒットでラップミュージックを一躍日本のポップシーンの第一線へと押し上げた、EAST END X YURI。『DA・YO・NE』はハードコアラップの対極にある。彼らのラップは銃や売春婦といった英米でありがちなテーマの絶叫とは違い、元気でほがらかな普通の男の子女の子の話題が多い。また、同曲は大阪版の『SO・YA・NA』など他のユニットによる数種類の方言バージョンでも話題を呼んだ。『DA・YO・NE』のヒット以前、既に日本のラップアーティストは日本版アメリカンラップをほぼ完成させつつあった。しかし、アメリカとの社会性の違いから、日本のキッズはアメリカのスタイルをそのまま受け入れることに抵抗を感じていたのではないかと、エピックソニーのあるスタッフは指摘をする。『DA・YO・NE』の歌詞は日本のティーンの気楽な会話そのもの。無理なく彼らに受け入れられたのではと、氏は語る。

VIBRASTONE DASSEN TRIO

Fronted by Haruo Chikada, VibraStone is a collection of top-notch musicians who are obviously playing the kind of music they like. Their live shows are intense—you're guaranteed to work up a sweat.

Chikada has been in the vanguard of Japanese pop music ever since making his debut in 1975, working in bands such as Haruo-phone and President BPM. Of VibraStone, Chikada says, "This is the band for which I've been searching for 20 years."

What makes VibraStone different from other Japanese hip-hop units is that the music is real—there are no tapes or other effects. Another unique aspect of the band is its "mass rapping."

"By 'mass-rap,' I mean rapping by all the band members together," explains Chikada. "This is our unique way of doing rap music. This style may begin to sound kind of stupid, but it's our uniqueness. Each member, including those without solo rap parts, has to put the same weight both on playing their instrument and rapping. This is what the band is all about."

While many Japanese rappers try the hardest to be as cool and heavy as the American role models, others take a more lighthearted approach. Osaka's Dassen Trio are a case in point. Their style is based on Osaka-style *owarai* comedy shtick. They're produced by Yoshimoto Kogyo, a long-established Osaka production company that in the mid-'90s branched out into cutting-edge fields like rap.

Another Japanese rap act to emphasize comedy in its act is the duo Geisha Girls, who despite their name, are in fact male.

多くのグループがアメリカのラッパーを真似しくクールになろうとする中、わざと軽いノリを追及しているのが大阪出身の脱線３。所属会社である吉本興業は90年代中期よりラップなど最先端の音楽を手がけている。ステージではディレイやエフェクト等を一切使わないビブラストーンは他のヒップホップバンドとは一線を画す。彼等

彼等のグループのベースにはドタバタのお笑いがある。ステージでディレイやエフェクト等を一切使わないビブラストーンは他のヒップホップバンドとは一線を画す。彼等の合唱スタイルのラップもユニーク。

CIBO MATTO

...panese women performing songs in ...acky English about food—Shonen ...ife, right? No, we're talking about Cibo ...atto, a duo comprising two Japanese ...sidents (Yuka Honda and Miho Hatori) ... New York's Lower East Side, whose ...iquely bizarre spin on rap and pop ...usic in general landed them a major-...bel deal and critical acclaim in both the ...S. and Japan.

Check out these lyrics from the rap ...now Your Chicken," which originally ...peared on their eponymous 1995 ...panese mini-album:

I know my chicken.

ou got to know your chicken. ...pare the ...od and ...poil the ...ick. ...efore you ...o and ...hit a brick.

While rap is only one ingredient in ...bo Matto's surreal sonic stew, food ...a constantly recurring metaphor in ...eir songs.

Honda and Hatori are also involved ... a side project called Butter 08, a group ...ose other members are Mike Mills, ...ck Lee, and Russell Simins. So far, ...ey've released one album on the ...astie Boys' Grand Royal label.

Of the two, Honda (keyboards/sampler ... s the most extensive résumé, having ...ayed in a wide variety of New York–...sed groups since the late '80s. She's ...ayed with no-waver Arto Lindsay, ...ant-garde jazzman Dave Douglas, the ...nk band Leitoh Lychee, and John ...rn's Cobra, in addition to forays into ...-hop, acid jazz, and soul.

m.c. A.T.

One of Japan's most popular rappers, m.c. A.T. (the "A.T." stands for Akio Togashi) has brought a pop sensibility to the medium while maintaining a modicum of street credibility. In his lyrics, the macho posturing of rap is balanced by a strong romantic streak, as in "Oh! My Precious":

I know how to dry one's tears. Cause I know the first setback and one's sadness over it. In your life, you can't overcome problems just by being good and sweet. You need a man just like me, don't you?

Obviously, a lot of the impact is lost in translation, but in Japanese, m.c. A.T.'s lyrics give voice to the feelings of young people preoccupied with trials and tribulations of love—not guns, crack, and 'hos.

型破りな英語で食べ物について歌う女性バンド。少年ナイフ？　と思いがちだが、チボマットである。少女達は不思議なラップとポップのミックスで、メジャーとの契約と高い評価を勝ち取った。日本でも指折りの人気を誇るラッパー、m.c.AT。ラップが本来持つストリート的な説得力を残しつつポップに仕上げることができる彼の歌は、NY ロウアーイースト在住の日本人デュオ。彼女達は不思議なラップとポップのミックスで、銃やドラッグではなく「愛」やがむしゃらな若者の気持ちを歌う。

97

DJ HOND

While acts like East End X Yuri and Dassen Trio serve up what could be called rap lite, DJ Honda has elected to follow a much less commercially oriented path. He enlists the talents of stateside rappers such as Fat Joe, Gangstarr, and the Beatnuts to create a hard-core hip-hop sound.

Honda—who doesn't actually rap himself—says he decided to work with stateside rappers because in his book, Japanese rappers still just don't have what it takes.

"Japanese rap has only recently developed into a major scene," explains the turntable/console whiz in his deep, husky voice. "It will change and develop its style in the future, just like American rap did from old-school to new-school. But at this point, I don't know any rappers in Japan who can rap with the groove. If there was one, I would have asked him to rap for me."

DJ Honda's eponymous debut album came out on the Sony Records label in mid-1995 and was released in the U.S. by Relativity Records in spring 1996, becoming the first release by a Japanese hip-hop artist to attract attention in the American market. It reached no. 90 on Billboard's R&B chart. While not recording or doing promotion in the U.S., Honda keeps busy with production work back in Japan.

Honda has always been something of an outsider, from the time he arrived in Tokyo from his native Hokkaido (Japan's northernmost island—not usually considered a hotbed of hip-hop culture) in the early '80s. He found a job at a disco and to his surprise found himself asked to work as a DJ—a possibility he'd never considered.

"That's where I learned not only about black music, but also about techno, rock, and other styles," Honda recalls. "I was only a disco DJ, and then I worked my way up to where I am now."

At the beginning of the '90s, Honda started doing remixing and production work for a Tokyo-based indie label. In 1992 he was one of the DJs going system-to-system in New York's Battle for World Supremacy event, which is where he met many of the American rappers featured on his debut album.

"The artists I recorded with are all friends of mine," Honda explains. "I'd known what they were doing, and they liked the sound I was doing. I didn't want to work with people I don't know."

Honda's deep, pulsating grooves are matched in intensity by the hard-core lyrics the crew of American rappers he assembled for the project, including Biz Markie, Redman, Common Sense and Erick Sermon, have provided.

"DJ Honda is one of the realest and illest niggas that I've ever worked with, and what's really ill is that he's Japanese!" exclaims Fat Joe.

"Not only does DJ Honda have skills as a DJ, but he's excellent from a production standpoint as well. There are only a few people out there who can really say that," say the Beatnuts.

Honda says he doesn't have a problem communicating with American rappers. "To me, the sound is much more important than the words or message. That's why I'm a DJ, a remixer, and a producer. Hip-hop is a style beyond country, culture, or color."

Honda's next release after *DJ Honda* was *DJ Honda Remixes*, comprising his versions of tracks by Columbia and Relativity artists such as Cypress Hill, Common Sense, and Fat Joe.

"Hip-hop music has to have a groove in the sound, but Japanese is a language with its own rhythm. If they find a way to put those two different things together, that's probably when the Japanese hip-hop scene will get really interesting."

East End X Yuri や脱線3が軽いラップ路線を選ぶ一方で、DJ Honda は商業路線とはかけ離れた道を進んでいる。自身で歌わず米ラッパー達と共にハードコアなヒップホップを展開中。将来性はあるものの、日本のラッパーはまだグルーヴを理解していないと Honda は言う。北海道出身の彼は上京後ディスコDJとしてスタート、90年代初頭に渡米、DJ大会で多くのラッパー達と出会う。Honda のディープに脈打つグルーヴはビズ・マーキー、レッドマンといったラッパー達のハードな歌詞としっくりいった様だ。ビートナッツは制作面での能力を高く評価。ビートナッツは国や文化、人種を超えた音楽。詞よりも音が大切であり、だからこそ自分はDJだと言い切る。また、Honda にとってはヒップホップはグルーヴがなければならないし、日本語には独特のリズムがある。この二つを旨く融合する道を見つけたとき、日本のヒップホップは面白くなるだろうと語る。

OSAKA AND THE SOUNDS OF JAPAN'S WILD WEST

第2の都市大阪はお世辞にも美しく整っているとは言えないが、それは大阪人の気取らない気質に反映されている。「こんにちわ」ではなく「もうかってまっか」と挨拶し、彼等ほど地元を誇りに思っている人々もいない。大阪から飛び出した女性3人組少年ナイフが代弁するように大阪は常にベストなのである。勿論、彼女達は強烈に個性的な大阪が生み出したバンドの一つにすぎない。大阪 vs 東京はサンフランシスコ vs ニューヨークに似ているかもしれない。大阪のバンドは独立心が旺盛で、メジャー契約後もレコード会社の指図によってスタイルを変えない。多くのバンドはスターになることを目的には活動をしていないと在阪プロダクション会社プロデューサー潮田洋一は語る。ヒットねらい東京のバンドはスタイルまで変えるのでつまらないと言う。それに対し、大阪のバンドは「黙って聞け！」という態度に溢れ、観客もそのパワーみなぎるスタイルに魅きつけられているのだ。

North East South West

Osaka, Japan's 2nd City,

is not pretty. In fact, it's a D UMP: the kind of place that gives urban sp r aw l a bad name.

Its lack of any pretensions to being included in any 10 Most Beautiful Cities in the World list is reflected in the direct, no-bullshit attitude of its citizens. Instead of the standard Japanese greeting *konnichiwa* ("good day"), Osakans are more likely to use the more earthy *mohkatte makka*?—literally, "Are you making money?"

They're also fiercely proud of their city. In the immortal words of Shonen Knife, the best female power-pop trio ever to come out of the western Japanese metropolis:

I have been to LONDON one time
I have been to HONG KONG one time
Everywhere in the world is good
But Osaka is the best town
Osaka is the best town.

—"My Favorite Town"; lyrics by Naoko Yamano

Shonen Knife is just one of the many innovative and sometimes downright weird bands to have come out of the Osaka area's fervid musical scene. For Osaka musicians, there's no question: the west is best.

"Osaka bands are very independent," explains Mari Sato of Osaka production company Music Stuff, trying to be heard over the din as one of her acts sees how far into the red their equipment's db meters can go. "Even after they're signed to major labels they don't change their style. They don't like to be told by record companies or management what to do or not to do." Says Tokyo-based music writer Kaz Fukatsu: "Osaka bands are freer, more open—it's like San Francisco versus New York in the U.S. San Francisco and Osaka are the more 'experimental' cities for music."

"There are a lot of bands in Osaka who are not playing music with the idea of being stars," claims Yoichi Shioda, executive producer at Osaka production house Pop Company. "To me Tokyo isn't interesting, because it seems like the bands there are only thinking about scoring a hit. If the audience doesn't like their music, they'll quickly change their style. But with Osaka bands, it's more like 'Shut up and listen to how great we are!' Osaka audiences like that powerful style."

少年ナイフ

For Shonen Knife, the world is divided into two basic categories: Osaka and Everywhere Else.

AKA

"For us, Tokyo seems as far away as the United States," says Naoko Yamano, Shonen Knife's main vocalist/ songwriter and de facto leader.

Shonen Knife, the band that made the world safe for songs about flying jelly beans, household cleaning liquid, and insect collecting, is Osaka's best known musical export. Their music is a strange but endearing amalgam of the Ramones, the Ronettes, and the Beatles (and, some would say, the Shaggs) as well as their own comically kitsch sensibility. Over the years the female trio has moved from being so-bad-they're-good to a more polished style, without losing their charm or sense of humor.

The Shonen Knife story begins in Osaka in 1982, when sisters Naoko (guitar, vocals) and Atsuko Yamano (drums, vocals) and friend Michie Nakatani (bass, vocals) got together to play music as a hobby after they'd entered the work force as "office ladies"—the Japanese-English term for female clerical staff.

They kept working at their day jobs while releasing a series of records on Osaka independent label Zero Records, which subsequently signed licensing deals with various foreign indies. Word about the band spread among indie-music fans overseas, especially after the 1991 release of *Every Band Has a Shonen Knife Who Loves Them*, a collection of Shonen Knife covers by alternative acts such as White Flag and Redd Kross.

Overseas inquiries about Shonen Knife caught the attention of Keith Cahoon, managing director of Tower Records Far East. Cahoon brought the band to the attention of Page Porrazzo, at that time director of the international department for Virgin Music Japan, who became convinced the band had potential. "They had a unique sensibility, good songs, and the ability to appeal to people," Porrazzo says. "The problem was they weren't being recorded properly."

The band's first U.S. tour in the summer of 1991, including a date at CBGB's in New York, resulted in an MTV news spot and coverage in *The New York Times*, among other media. After returning to Japan, Shonen Knife and Virgin Music signed a publishing and management deal, which led to major-label record contracts in Japan, North America, and Europe.

少年ナイフにとって世界は大阪かその他という2通りしかない。東京もアメリカも同じくらい遠い場所らしい。「私たちにとって世界で最も世界に知られているバンド。そのサウンドは奇妙ながらもラモーンズやビートルズを彷彿させ、独特のキッチュな感覚が加わっている。バンドは山野直子（ギター）と山野敦子（ドラム）の姉妹、友人の中谷美智子（ベース）ら3人のOLのアフター5の趣味として始まった。地元大阪のインディーズレーベルZEROから数枚のレコードをリリースした後、海外のレーベルとも契約。91年夏には初のアメリカツアーが成功、帰国と同時にヴァージンレコードと契約。同年秋にニルヴァーナのUKツアーのオープニングを務め、その名は海外インディーズ業界に知れ渡った。91年夏に『Every Band Has a Shonen Knife Who Loves Them』というオルタナ系ロックバンドのカバー集により、その奥に込められた風刺が聴き逃されてしまう少年ナイフ。時としてその無邪気な英語の歌詞に注目が集まり、その奥に込められた風刺が聴き逃されてしまう少年ナイフ。『Space Christmas』もUKインディーズシングルチャートのトップへと登り詰めた。93年にリリースし、海外で十万枚セールスを上げた『Rock Animal』後、ヴァージンとの意見の違いがあり3年のブランクを経て96年春に出した『Brand New Knife』は自分達の音楽を決して変えることのない大阪バンド・少年ナイフらしさに溢れている。メンバーの直子は、メロディーにのせやすい英語の詞を作った後に日本語の詞を作るというが、その音楽は、日本人向けでもアメリカ人向けでもなく、「少年ナイフな人々」のために作っていると彼女はいう。

Shonen Knife

Favorites

1.(Love Is Like A) Heat wave / 2.Don't Hurt My Little Sister
3.Till The End Of The Day / 4.Boys
5.Goose Steppin' Mama

Blue eyes, blond hair
Tight body, long legs
She's glamorous
She's welcomed by boys
Oh, sexy girl! Oh, sexy girl! Oh, sexy gir
I wanna be Twist Barbie...

Shonen Knife's next break came in late November 1991, when they were chosen as a support act on Nirvana's three-week U.K. tour. When Nirvana suddenly broke big, Shonen Knife found themselves riding the Seattle group's coattails, and their single "Space Christmas" went to the top of the British indie singles chart.

In 1992 they made their major-label debut in Japan with the album *Let's Knife,* which was also released overseas. Their best-selling album to date, 1993's *Rock Animals,* sold a total of about 100,000 copies outside of Japan, compared with roughly 50,000 at home.

While overseas critics patronizingly seized on their wonky English, many missed the thought that goes into the band's seemingly lightweight lyrics.

For example, at first glance, "Twist Barbie" from *Let's Knife* is merely a paean to the Barbie doll, but it's also an ironic commentary on the way Asian women are confronted by Western concepts of female beauty:

Following the 1993 release of *Rock*

Animals, Shonen Knife went nearly three years without putting out a new album. In the fast-paced world of Japanese pop, that amounts to career suicide. But true to its self-reliant Osakan spirit, Shonen Knife was determined to chart its own course in the music biz.

In early 1994, the band did a 28-date North American tour to support the release of *Rock Animals.* Later the same year Shonen Knife took part in the Lollapalooza alternative-rock tour of the U.S. and Canada. And they recorded an inspired version of the Carpenters' "Top of the World" for the *If I Were a Carpenter* tribute album, which came out in 1994.

In spring 1996, that track was chosen by Microsoft as the theme song for a TV ad campaign that aired in the U.S. and

Japan—which certainly didn't have a negative effect on the band members' bank accounts.

Meanwhile, back in Japan, the trio continued to play live dates, filmed a beer commercial, and were the subject of an NHK TV documentary, while squeezing into whatever time they had left over rehearsals and writing new songs.

Consigned by many to the has-been-novelty-act category, after the female trio finally did bounce back with a new album in 1996, they did it in the style. The impressive album was appropriately titled *Brand New Knife.*

"We don't make our music for American or Japanese people—we make our music for Shonen Knife people," Naoko says.

At first, the Nelories seem similar to Shonen Knife: a girl band from western Japan signing bizarre pop songs in screwy English. But the Nelories, a duo who hail from the ancient Japanese capital of Nara, have a slightly more cerebral edge than Shonen Knife. Take these lines from "Neutral Blue," for example, set to the duo's trademark guitar/accordion accompaniment:

"You were a son of neutral blue It was the color of your talking But now, never will I hear your voice as I used to do."

Inscrutable, or just plain weird? The Nelories—Jun Kirihara and Kazumi Kubo—are part of the same offbeat, surreal tradition that spawned '80s cult faves the Frank Chickens. Their quirky, English-language songs are reminiscent of Shonen Knife, but instead of a garage-band sound, the Nelories favor an almost minimalist style, which is dominated by Kirihara's accordion, backed by Kubo's guitar, plus bass and drums.

Vocalist Kirihara's lyrics are surreal meditations on subjects ranging from Japanese female tourists shopping overseas to the depressing urban landscape of "No Love Lost": "Broken bicycle/Crushed fruit on the street/The clouds in the sky don't seem nice at all."

The Nelories have gained a loyal cult following in Britain, where they have played live gigs as well as recorded a session for Radio One's John Peel. Their continuing modest success shows that the group is starting to mature into something that's more than a flash in the rice cooker.

The Nelories

英語で歌う関西系女性バンド、ネロリーズは一見したところ、少年ナイフ2世かと思われそうだが、古都奈良出身のこのデュオの方がさらに摩訶不思議。栗原淳と久保和美が作り出す変わった英語の歌詞は少年ナイフを彷彿させるが、栗原のアコーディオンをサポートする久保のギターにベースとドラムがよりミニマリストな印象。英国で熱狂的なファンを獲得し、ジョン・ピールのセッションにも参加。爆発的ではないが安定した活躍は本物を感じさせる。

Shiro Amamiya

Osaka-based DJ/producer Shiro Amamiya, best known outside Japan for his work with dance-music unit Ecstasy Boys, went to New York in 1988 to work and study.

"Everybody was so surprised when I went to New York instead of Tokyo," says Amamiya, who was the DJ at the 1993 New Music Seminar's Psycho Nite Japanese music showcase. "But I thought if I went to Tokyo, I would disappear there."

He says he feels vindicated now that his music is being released overseas and being exported to Japan with that vital "foreign" cachet attached to it.

While Shonen Knife's songs deal with subjects like flying jelly bean attacks and food poisoning from eating spoiled oysters, Amamiya's music is on another plane altogether.

"I think a 'spiritual music' movement is beginning," explains Amamiya during an interview at Osaka's Space for Child recording studio.

To prove his point, Amamiya plays back a rough mix of his latest project, *Satori*, which combines house-style synthesized sounds, Indian percussion, and multilingual vocals, resulting in a rich, hypnotic aural tapestry.

"My dream is to go to Tibet and make a dance track with monks there," he says as the swirling, pulsating sound of a cut called "Tibet Is" fills the minuscule studio control room.

"I think Osaka has a little more rhythm than Tokyo," says Amamiya. Another key difference between the two rival cities' club scenes, he says, is that Osaka DJs are more relaxed and less uptight about cooperating with each other.

"Here, we don't have to care so much about what other people think," Amamiya says. "In Tokyo, the DJs always follow New York or London. They won't even play their own records in the clubs. Tokyo is too fashionable — the cycles are too fast."

But as the examples of Amamiya, Shonen Knife, and the Nelories show, bypassing Tokyo and taking one's wares overseas can be the best way to go — something which appeals to Osakans' strong sense of local pride and identity.

"Lots of people from the Osaka area go directly to the U.S., because they're not interested in the Tokyo music scene," says Fukatsu.

Notes Shioda: "I don't think Tokyo-based record companies would mind signing Osaka bands, but they just don't take the time to come down here to discover talent."

106

大阪を拠点に活躍するDJ LAMA天宮志龍は海外では88年にNYで活動したエクスタシー・ボーイズと言った方が通りが良いかもしれない。ロンドンやパリが英国やフランスにとってそうであるように、東京は紛れもなく日本の中心でありメジャーレコード会社が本社を構え、多くのアーティストは東京で成功する事を目指す。しかし天宮や少年ナイフ、ネロリーズのように東京を通り越て海外に直接出ていく事は、関西人であることのプライドの高さを表わしている。

Ulfuls

The most recent examples of Osaka's brash rock 'n' roll tradition are two bands with the unlikely names of the Ulfuls and Sha Ram Q.

You've got to like a group whose members have nutzo names like Tortoise Matsumoto and John B. Chopper. We're talking about the Ulfuls, one of the more surprising success stories on the Japanese music scene in 1996.

This four-member band, which got started in Osaka in 1988, specializes in manic, in-your-face comedy-rock. The video of their hit tune "Gattsu daze!!" is a wicked send-up of Japanese cinematic clichés, with ninjas, geishas, samurai and other Edo-period characters cavorting madly in what looks like a Kabuki show choreographed by Spike Jones. Totally insane.

The band's name, by the way, comes from the word "soulful," with the letters "so" removed. Don't ask me why.

Sha Ram Q

Sha Ram Q are more in the "visual rock" vein than the Ulfuls, but in their own way are just as wackily eccentric. Smoke bombs, strange white liquids spurting out from band members' bodies, and strange hairstyles are just some of the gimmicks the band uses. Oh, yes, they also play music—of the pop-rock variety.

阪ロックの流れを汲む最近のバンドといえばウルフルズとシャ乱Q。トータス松本やジョン・B・チョッパーという名前のメンバーがいるバンドを嫌いになれる人はいないだろう。それが96年意外性NO.1のサクセスストーリー、ウルフルズである。忍者、芸者、侍が飛び交うビデオ「ガッツだぜ！」は必見。シャ乱Qはウルフルズよりも「ビジュアル系」だが、それも彼等なりのやり方でだ。音楽はポップロック系とでも言うべきか

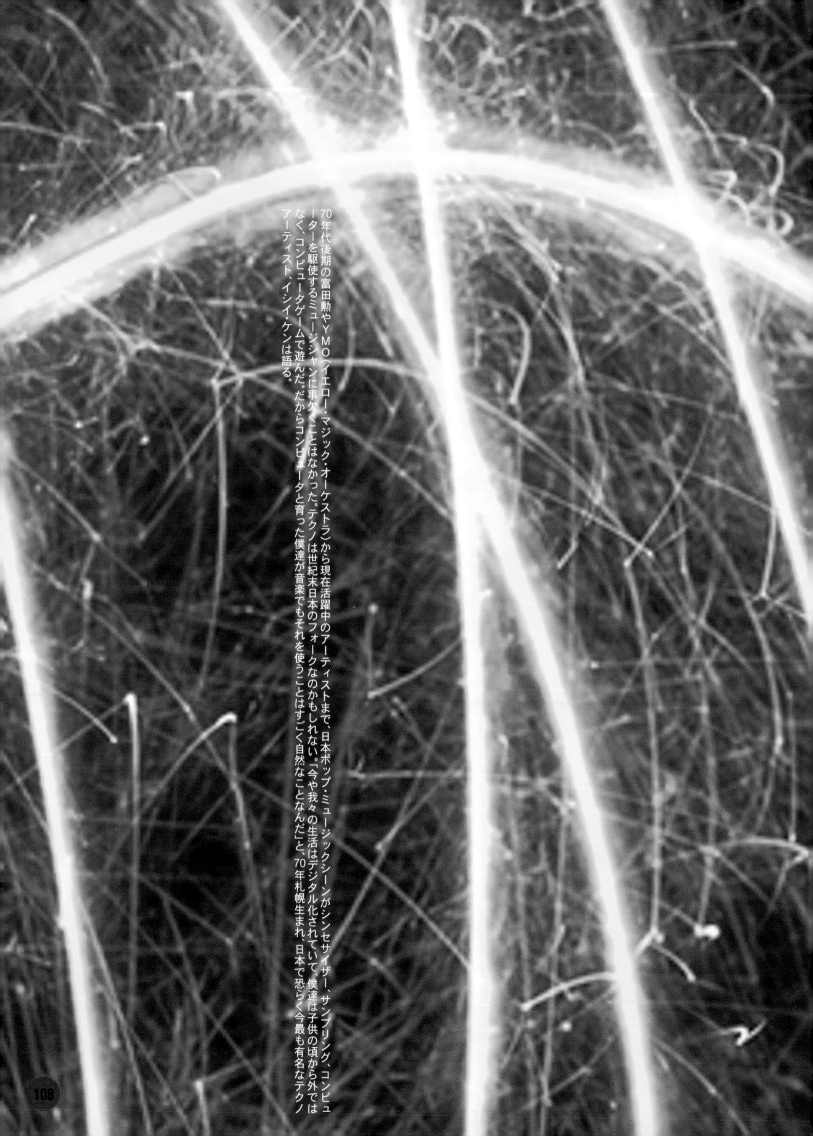

70年代後期の富田勲やYMO（イエロー・マジック・オーケストラ）から現在活躍中のアーティストまで、日本ポップ・ミュージックシーンがシンセサイザー、サンプリング、コンピューターを駆使するミュージシャンに事欠くことはなかった。テクノは世紀末日本のフォークなのかもしれない。「今や我々の生活はデジタル化されていて、僕達は子供の頃から外ではなく、コンピュータゲームで遊んだ。だからコンピュータと育った僕達が音楽でもそれを使うことはすごく自然なことなんだ」と、70年札幌生まれ、日本で恐らく今最も有名なテクノアーティスト、イシイ・ケンは語る。

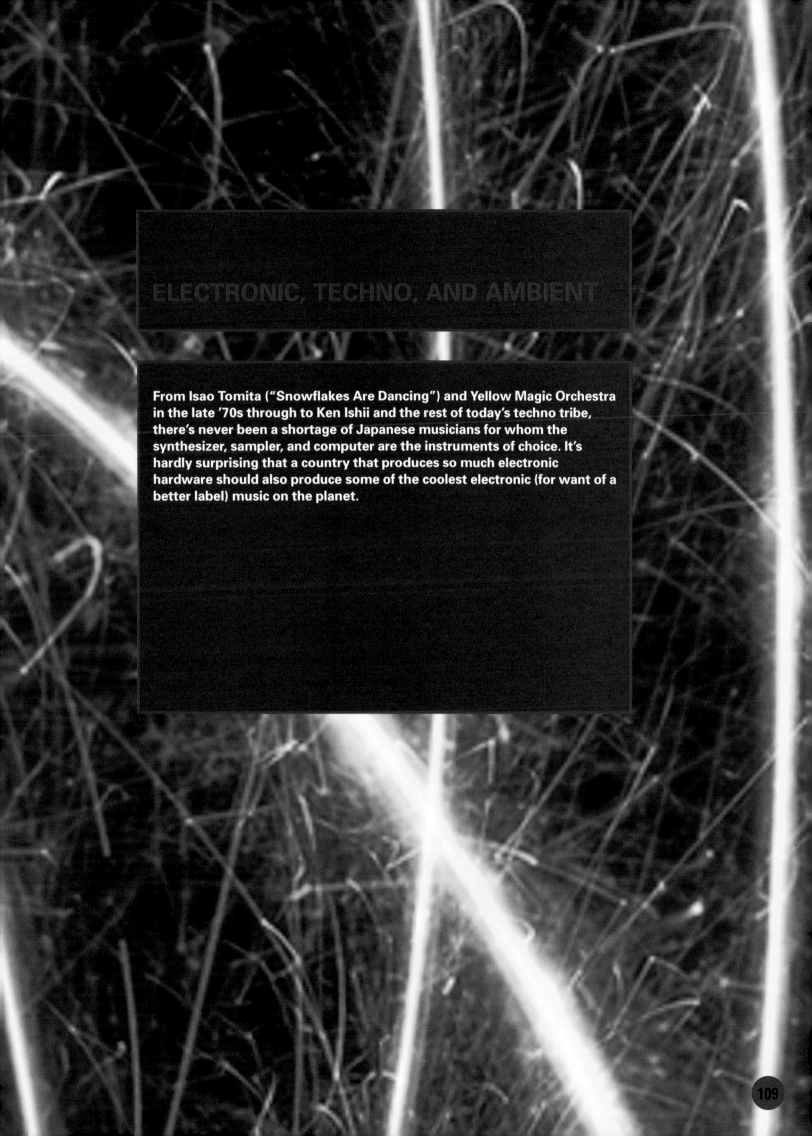

ELECTRONIC, TECHNO, AND AMBIENT

From Isao Tomita ("Snowflakes Are Dancing") and Yellow Magic Orchestra in the late '70s through to Ken Ishii and the rest of today's techno tribe, there's never been a shortage of Japanese musicians for whom the synthesizer, sampler, and computer are the instruments of choice. It's hardly surprising that a country that produces so much electronic hardware should also produce some of the coolest electronic (for want of a better label) music on the planet.

Ken Ishii

The do-it-yourself nature of the music is what attracted Ken Ishii to techno.

"The reason I started to make music was the possibility of doing everything on my own," Ken Ishii states matter-of-factly. "For me, the first motivation to make music was electronic music, and I didn't want to play in a band. My interest was always in the sounds made by machines or electronic equipment—I wasn't interested in the human voice," he says.

That doesn't mean his sonic vocabulary is limited to electronic sounds.

"Most young Japanese don't like traditional music—but not me. I put in any element of music which I've been listening to. I'm interested in Japanese traditional percussion or *gagaku* (ancient court music). It's impossible to find the same sort of thing in European music."

Back in 1992, though, Ishii's cybernetic musical vision was just a bit too far ahead of prevailing trends in Japan, so his first record deal was with Belgian techno label R & S Records.

"I was listening to imported records, so I knew the techno scene in Europe was becoming more active. When I started to make music, I wanted to release it in Japan, but there was no record company and no audience for me. R & S was my favorite label... so I mailed them my demo tape."

Ishii's first releases on R & S were the 12-inch singles "Garden on the Palm," "Pneuma," "Deep Sleep,"

and "Tangled Notes." In 1994 R & S released Ishii's first full-length album, *Innerelements*, comprising earlier releases and new material.

"I don't make dance music only," says the soft-spoken Ishii. "So I think my music is best described as electronic music."

In 1995, Sony Records licensed what was then Ishii's latest album, *Jelly Tones*, which in Japan also included a CD-ROM titled *Extra*, featuring a nine-minute anime clip by Katsuhiro Otomo.

In it, a superhero-type character modeled on Ishii travels on an aerial scooter through a futuristic, neo-Asian cityscape populated by nasty humanoid types whom our hero dispatches to their doom as Ishii's brooding, driving music creates an atmosphere of mystery and danger. The music-video version of *Extra* was chosen as MTV Europe's 1996 Dance Video of the Year.

Apart from some samples, the sounds Ishii creates bear no relation to anything in the natural soundscape—like that of Britain's Aphex Twin, this is pure electronic music. Sometimes, on tracks like Jelly Tones' "Rusty Transparency," Ishii's music is dissonant and metallic, while on pieces like "Endless Season," from the same album, the mood is lush and haunting, reminiscent of Tangerine Dream or Klaus Schulze in their more lyrical moments. Keeping it all together are the relentless, metronomic rhythms of techno.

音楽を始めた当初からエレクトロニックサウンドの魅力にとりつかれ、「人間の肉声には興味がなかった」と言うイシイ・ケン。しかし、雅楽のような伝統的な音楽の影響も多大に受けていると本人は語る。ベルギーのテクノレーベル、R&Sでデビュー以来、ヨーロッパを中心にヒットを続け、1996年には、『Extra』のミュージックビデオがMTVヨーロッパのダンスビデオ部門で最優秀賞を受賞した。

The Liquid Room and the
beginning of the techno scene

The Liquid Room, a club in the heart of Tokyo's sleazy Kabukicho district, is the epicenter of Japanese techno.

At a Liquid Room gig, the stage is blocked off by a large screen on which a light show of pulsating, constantly changing imagery plays. It can only be described as psychedelic. The technoids who've arrived early mill about in front of the stage, waiting for something to happen.

The music coming out of the massive sound system gradually shifts gears from an almost subliminal electronic hum to a steady techno beat over which DJ Wada casts great sweeping washes of synthesized and sampled sound. Abandoning their pose of studied cool, the techno fans milling about the club begin to move to the music, and before long, the Liquid Room has become a vortex of sound, light, and bodies in motion.

One of the of the DJ's manning the turntables and electronic gizmos at the Liquid Room tonight is Tomoyaki Hirata, who doubles as chief editor of leading techno magazine *Loud*. It vies with rival publication *Ele-King* as the most authoritative guide to Japan's techno scene.

"I was really into the European techno scene around '91 and '92," recalls Hirata in relaxed, fluent English in his cubbyhole of an office in Tokyo's Shibuya. "I tried to import that scene to Japan but I didn't have any skill or knowledge about running or organizing a club or making records or being a DJ. I didn't know very much."

Hirata's enthusiasm got the better of him, though, and together with photographer Kenji Kubo, he began a series of techno events called Club Venus at the Liquid Room in 1993.

"At that time there wasn't such a big techno scene here," Hirata notes. "There were maybe only 300 people at the event. It was not an easy time.

"Then the club jazz music explosion happened here, but we were still struggling to make the techno scene bigger. *Remix* (a club-music magazine where Hirata then worked) got more jazz- and hip-hop-oriented. I think that was a good thing, but we loved techno and house, so that's why I started *Loud*."

日本のテクノの中核、歌舞伎町にあるクラブ、The Liquid Room。大きなスクリーンや照明器具。店内は演奏が始まるとすぐに大量の音と光、そして踊り狂う客であふれる。ターンテーブルを回すDJ、平田知昌はテクノ雑誌「Loud」の編集長という顔も持つ。彼は93年にLiquid RoomでテクノイベントClub Venusをスタートさせたが、当時のテクノシーンは今ほど熱くはなかったと回想する。

AVEX AND SONY/Denki Groove

テクノ普及にもっとも貢献した日本のレーベルといえば、群を抜いて Avex と Sony。ダンスミュージックを主に手がける Avex は 80 年代後半から 90 年代初頭にかけて、Juliana's のリミックスで日本にテクノの基盤を築いた。一方、Sony は『Mix-Up』シリーズをリリース。国内のアーティストから UFO や坂本龍一、海外からは Moby や Mr. Fingers などの曲を石野卓球らによるアレンジでリミックスした。

Avex and Sony have been way ahead of other Japanese record labels in popularizing techno.

Dance specialist Avex helped lay the groundwork for techno in Japan in the late '80s and early '90s with its immensely popular "Juliana's" compilations of techno-rave music licensed from overseas labels. More recently, Avex has concentrated on jungle, trance, and house, and hopes to release music by domestic techno artists in such sub-genres as psychedelic trance.

Sony has released a series of compilations titled *Mix-Up* in which artists such as Ishii, Jeff Mills, and Takkyu Ishino—who oversees the series—mutate Dand warp tracks by acts such as Japan's United Future Organization and Ryuichi

Sakamoto and foreign acts like Moby, Moebius-Plank-Neumeier, and Mr. Fingers, among others.

The *Mix-Up* albums come close to reproducing the electric atmosphere of a techno club where the DJ is really on. Each track builds and builds before blending seamlessly into the next selection, the sonic collage shifting in color and emphasis as the beats ebb and flow. Highly recommended.

Another crucial Japanese techno act is Denki Groove, whose leader is Ishino. Their March 1996 release, *Orange* (Ki/oon Sony), is Japan's best-selling techno title, having moved about 310,000 copies. Its success is best explained by the group's more pop-oriented sound.

RAINBOW 2000

電気グルーヴ

ウッドストックと見間違うような光景が繰り広げられた。ここは御殿場。96年夏のレインボー2000、テクノを一つのジャンルとして確立させたオールナイトレイブ。一万五千人が富士山近郊のこの地に集まり、駆り立てるようなリズムとドリーミーな雰囲気に酔った。60年代アメリカ音楽とこのテクノライブは似ている。モティーフが繰り返し使われ、レーザーショー、トリップ感、ラブ＆ピースや環境保護といったテーマが強調された。

A large field filled with thousands of brightly dressed, unconventional-looking people, swaying rhythmically as heavily amplified music and telltale verdant aromas fill the air.

Monterey 1967? Hyde Park 1968? Try Gotenba, Japan, Aug. 10, 1996. The occasion was Rainbow 2000, an ambitious all-night concert/rave/event that saw 15,000 people gather together to enjoy the driving rhythms and dreamy ambience created by Japanese techno artists including Ken Ishii, Takkyu Ishino, Tokyo Techno Tribe, and Something Wonderful.

There are more than a few parallels between Japan's techno tribe and the '60s counterculture. In both movements, music provides the leitmotif, along with light shows, hallucinogens, and an emphasis on values such as peace, love, and ecology—not to mention that indefinable collective "vibe." Rainbow 2000 marked Japanese techno's emergence from the underground, claims Jun Ochi of concert promotion company Tachyon, which organized the event.

"Reggae was underground in Japan for 10 or 15 years," says Ochi. "It was the same with jazz, rock, chanson—anything is underground in the beginning. The most exciting moment is when it breaks out and comes above ground. I like to be there when it happens, and this time, I found this was happening with techno."

AMBIENT & HARUOMI HOSONO

テクノあるところにアンビエントあり。日本も例外ではない。アンビエントの巨匠、細野晴臣。その名はJポップ史に幾度となく登場する。APRYL FOOLからはっぴいえんど、ティン・パン・アレー等、今やビンテージともいえるロックバンドを経て、78年には坂本龍一、高橋幸宏と共にYMOを結成、テクノポップというジャンルを確立した。以後もソロ活動やジョイントなどで多くのアルバムをリリースしている。細野はアナログ対デジタル論争も冷静に受けとめている。「僕はアナログ楽器で作る音同様、デジタル楽器が出す音も好きなんだ。デジタル機器ではアナログ調の温かい音が出せないという訳じゃない。結局、どう使いこなすかで決まってくるんだよ」と語る。ファンキーなダンス系から雅楽を取り入れたリラクゼーション物まで日本テクノの多様化は進む一方。Frogman、Sublime、Transonic、Subvoice、Trip Trap等々、各レーベルが個性を競いあっている。

Where there's techno, there's ambient music, and Japan is no exception. As any dedicated Tokyo clubgoer knows, techno and ambient are two sides of the same coin. The exhilaration and buzz of techno soon give way to ambient's chill-out vibe.

Ambient's leading Japanese advocate is Haruomi Hosono, who along with Ryuichi Sakamoto and Yukihiro Takahashi formed pioneering electro-pop group Yellow Magic Orchestra in the '70s. Hosono—who was a member of vintage Japanese rock bands such as Happy End, Apryl Fool, and Tin Pan Alley—is one of the most respected figures on the Japanese music scene. As you study the history of Japanese pop music, Hosono's name pops up again and again in all sorts of different contexts.

Through the years he's released many albums, either as a solo act or with various musicians, including Bill Laswell (the excellent *Interpieces Organization*, released on Teichiku Records in February 1996), singers Miyako Koda, Mimori Yusa, and Mishio Ogawa on the superb 1995 album *Love, Peace and Trance*, and most recently, female vocalist Miharu Koshi on the retro-ambient album *swing slow*. "Ambient is what I call pop now," says Hosono, whose calm, detached demeanor suggests ambience personified. "If there's something that excites kids just like rock music did before, it's ambient. It's a mixture of technology and shamanism."

If, for Ken Ishii, techno is the video-game generation's natural mode of musical expression, for Hosono, it's ambient.

"Because of the technology that's available now, young people can easily make these sounds," he says. "They play ambient because they think it's cool. For them, ambient is what rock music meant to people 20 years ago."

Hosono's comments carry a certain weight, given his status as one of the godfathers of Japanese pop.

"When I was a kid (Hosono was born in Tokyo in 1947), I was enthusiastic about rock," Hosono explains. "Rock was exciting back then."

When Hosono was in his teens, he was into artists like Neil Sedaka and Connie Francis. "Then it became '60s pop chart songs, such as the Beach Boys or hot rod music. I collected so many singles at that time. Then I was into West Coast psychedelic music like Moby Grape and Buffalo Springfield. That was when I was in Happy End. Those are my influences."

Happy End was one of the first groups to use the Japanese language intelligently and literately in a rock context. Until then, Japanese bands had tried to mimic the Anglo-American pop lyrical idiom in Japanese, with less-than-wonderful results. Happy End, despite its name, marked the beginning of a more mature, confident type of Japanese rock.

In the early '70s Hosono went solo, releasing albums like *Tropical Dandy* and *Paraiso*, which combined his West Coast sound influences with Polynesian percussion, synthesizers, and other assorted bits of sonic weirdness. He also started to be in demand as a producer.

In 1978 Hosono, Sakamoto, and Takahashi joined forces in Yellow Magic Orchestra (YMO), which along with groups like Germany's Kraftwerk, launched the genre known as techno-pop.

"There wasn't a long history of pop music in Japan, but all kinds of music and information about the music from around the world were always available to us," he points out. "Each of us had a great amount of information about music, so we were just having fun together with music… like the Ventures. When we debuted, there was punk and new wave, and the sound of YMO was light and frivolous, especially compared to the music coming from Europe at that time."

Hosono is not one of those artists who live to hear the deafening applause of their adoring fans.

"Live performances are so stressful," he explains. "I never enjoyed playing live. But the other day, I did a live show, playing percussion, at a small hotel near Lake Yamanaka (near Mt. Fuji) with a flute player in front of an audience of about 40 people. I really had fun. That's the kind of show I like."

The analog-vs.-digital debate fails to excite Hosono.

"As much as I like sounds made with analog equipment, I [also] like what you can do with digital equipment. You can still make warm, analog-like sounds with digital instruments. It's all up to how you use the machines.

"When I compose, I don't think too much about what I'm doing. Instead, many of my songs are impromptu. I just keep playing with lots of ad libs."

Like many other veteran figures on the Japanese music scene, Hosono is critical of Japanese pop music.

"It's still developing. It has just started—there's almost no history of pop music in Japan," he says. "There's no 'original' cultural background to rely on in Japan, although musicians and producers out there today do things a lot better than back when I started Happy End. Back then, nobody was any good at all. The only person I respect as a producer in Japan is Eiichi Ohtaki. He loves American pop songs from the '50s and the '60s, just like I do. We played together in Happy End."

KITARO

『The Light of the Spirit(魂の光)』や『Heaven and Earth(天と地)』といったアルバムタイトルがエキゾチックで霊的な喜多郎の音楽を象徴している。1978年に初のソロアルバムをリリース。以後もアメリカに住み活動を続けている。若い頃はピンクフロイドやキングクリムゾンなどを聴いていた彼も、自分の音楽を作り始めてからは他の音楽はほとんど聴かなくなったと語る。

Album titles like *The Light of the Spirit*, *Heaven and Earth* and *Mandala* offer more than a hint of where keyboardist Kitaro's coming from.

"I don't need to try to be spiritual or exotic," emphasizes Kitaro, whose wispy beard and piercing eyes lend him the aura of an Oriental sage. "It comes from me naturally."

Kitaro's cosmic image has helped him establish a solid niche in the American contemporary instrumental, aka New Age, market. Kitaro, who released his first solo album back in 1978, lives in the college town of Boulder, Colorado. He says that living in the United States has helped him concentrate more effectively on the American market.

"I like to compose and perform with an orchestra, but sometimes it's too expensive and takes time," says Kitaro. "The sound is so nice, sitting in front of a 100-piece orchestra, totally perfect, 3-D stereo—real sound."

That's a quality today's digital synthesizers lack, Kitaro complains. "The sound is horrible. I'm still using analog synthesizers (a 20-year-old Mini-Moog, a Korg 700, and a Korg 800), because I can control them better. They're much quicker and have more flexibility."

Kitaro started his musical career in the late '60s as a member of the Far East Family Band, first on guitar and later on bass. That band broke up in the early '70s after recording an album at Virgin Records' Oxfordshire, U.K., studio with German space-rock supremo Klaus Schulze in the producer's chair.

"I listened to British rock when I was a kid," Kitaro recalls. "Then Pink Floyd, King Crimson, Mike Oldfield—many kinds of progressive rock. Then I started creating my own sound. When I started doing my own thing, I almost stopped listening to other music."

The result has been a series of instrumental albums with strong Asian influences, such as Kitaro's two 1980 releases based on the theme of the ancient Silk Road trade route between Europe and the Far East, and 1990's *Kojiki*, which took Japan's creation myths as its subject. In 1993 he composed the soundtrack for Oliver Stone's film *Heaven and Earth*, which earned him a Golden Globe award.

Kitaro's music remains an acquired taste. Its Eastern exoticism appeals to the fern-bar set, but for others it's insufferably bombastic. Love him or hate him, the fact remains that Kitaro is one of the few Japanese musicians to have a lasting impact outside his native country.

'Techno Lolita'
and the Eccentric Opera

Hiroki Okano

岡野が手がけるテクノロリータ、篠原ともえ。彼女によってテクノをキッズに広める狙いがあるという。更に奇妙な東京芸大出身
の3人組Eccentric Opera。1996年のデビューアルバムにはテクノ調アレンジの「アヴェマリヤ」などが収録されている。日本テクノは
これからも進化していくだろう。一方、アンビエントの革新家は岡野弘幹。千個以上の風鈴を屋久島などに設置したレコーディン
グ等で有名。

Takkyu Ishino's latest project is producing the debut album of Tomoe Shinohara, a young female singer whom the label describes as a "very lovely techno Lolita."

The idea, explains Harry Yoshida of Ki/oon Sony, is for Shinohara to help make techno fashionable with young kids.

As if the idea of "techno Lolita" weren't strange enough, one Japanese act has attempted an unlikely fusion of techno and—wait for it—opera. The three members of the appropriately named Eccentric Opera are all graduates of the prestigious Tokyo National University of Fine Arts and Music. Their eponymous 1996 debut album on Epic/Sony includes technoized versions of selections from Handel's "Hallelujah" chorus, Puccini's "Madame Butterfly" and Schubert's "Ave Maria." The trio's visual style suggests something from a kinky leather bar more than grand opera. Eccentric is definitely the operative word here, and it remains to be seen whether the group will prove to be more than a novelty act.

Pretty well everybody you talk to here expects Japan's homegrown techno scene to keep growing.

"I think the Japanese scene is going to get bigger," says Masakazu "Hiro" Hiroishi, product manager at Sony Records' Office 7 section, who is

credited by many with putting Sony in the forefront of the Japanese techno boom. "But the concept of techno, the sound itself, is going to develop. I think it will be more funky, more groove-oriented, with more of a rock attitude. And there will be more emphasis on artists who can perform their music live."

One of Japan's most innovative ambient artists is Osaka-based keyboardist Hiroki Okano, whose gently soothing music overlaps with the slippery genre known as New Age. Okano has made a name for himself with his unique wind-bell installations, in which he places as many as 1,000 wind bells in a given location (Japan's Yakushima Island and Britain's Glastonbury, for example), and lets Mother Nature do the rest. His 1993 album, *Music of Wind*, was recorded on-site in Yakushima's primeval forest, and besides the bells, the album contains sounds such as birds and insects. A chart in the beautifully produced liner notes shows where these "musicians," as Okano describes them, can be heard on the album.

Ryuichi Sakamoto

Emperor (for which he won an Oscar, a Grammy, and a Golden Globe award) have made him perhaps the best known Japanese musician internationally—unless you count Yoko Ono. Artists Sakamoto has collaborated with include David Bowie, Youssou N'dour, David Byrne, Brian Eno, and David Sylvian.

Interviewed at a recording studio in western Tokyo suburbs, Sakamoto, who for the last few years has lived in New York, is scathing when it comes to the Japanese music scene.

"To me, the market is still very closed. And Japanese pop music sounds like it's made (only) for Japanese people. I listen to Japanese pop music out of sociological interest, not particularly for musical reasons.

"Look at Peter Gabriel—he puts out

representative of Japan. This was not my job," he laughs". The good thing is that through my activities in YMO, I met a lot of people. I did a lot of projects."

In 1993 YMO reunited for one album and a tour. Afterwards, Sakamoto was quoted as saying that the trio's new music was "too techno," which made many people wonder why he bothered with the project at all.

"There were tons of rumors about YMO reuniting and we kind of had pressure...from people, from fans," says Sakamoto after a long pause. *"It was very hard to find something we could share, because we'd been having different times for ten years and we were so far away [from each other]. We were like three different novelists writing one*

yuichi Sakamoto's academic background—he has a master's degree in electronic and ethnic music—and his serious demeanor have earned him the nickname "kyoju" (the professor). He first came to the public's attention when in 1978 he, Haruomi Hosono, and Yukihiro Takahashi formed Yellow Magic Orchestra. Over the next five years YMO released 11 albums and developed a techno-pop style that was and continues to be enormously influential.

The YMO legacy, plus Sakamoto's soundtrack work on films such as *Merry Christmas, Mr. Lawrence* and *The Last*

an album every five years. For artistic reasons, he needs that long to put out one album. But he sells a lot, so he can do that. It's such a difference compared with (Tetsuya) Komuro. That makes the quality of Japanese pop low."

Sakamoto puts the YMO phenomenon in historical context.

"At the time (of YMO's debut), there were many products from Japan going to the West. Like Honda cars and Comme des Garcons clothes. What we were doing symbolized those things from Japan. [But I didn't feel like] I was an ambassador or

novel. It's like Ryu Murakami, Haruki Murakami, and Banana Yoshimoto writing one novel together."

In 1996 Sakamoto released an album called, prosaically enough, *1996*, comprising pieces he'd written during various parts of his prolific career and performed in a violin-cello-piano format, with Sakamoto himself playing the latter instrument. It's an elegant, austerely beautiful introduction to his work, and led to questions about Sakamoto's long-term "serious" musical ambitions.

"I'll be able to write opera, symphonies,

soundtracks—serious music—when I get much older. I don't want to keep doing pop music when I'm 60—like Mick Jagger. If you say Brian Eno's music is a kind of pop music, that's what I'll be doing when I get into my sixties. But not dancing on stage. To me, the attitude of Eric Clapton is much more acceptable than Mick Jagger's.

"[One possibility is] a multimedia opera using a lot of people, even other writers, composers, and individual artists. All music is very close to me and generally I don't care about genres. I listen to anything. I create almost any kind of music. I understand that sometimes people might be confused about what I am. That's why I kind of focus on what I'm doing. But then I get bored with what I'm doing."

Bertolucci so much."

What about the heavy makeup on the character he played in *Merry Christmas, Mr. Lawrence?*

"That was strange... a Japanese officer with makeup like that! That was the makeup artist's idea, and the director, Oshima, liked it very much. Of course it wasn't a documentary film, it was a kind of fantasy between a Japanese soldier and an English soldier. Love between them. So it's OK. It's like a Fellini film."

Sakamoto, unlike many other Japanese musicians, is quite frank when it comes to the subject of drugs and music.

"In the '60s, when I was a teenager, I was sort of a hippie. I liked to do them.

When composing, Sakamoto sometimes starts with a basic groove or tape loop, to which he gradually adds other elements. Other times, he starts with the melody.

"I get ideas and store them in a computer, and when I have more time I drag those small pieces and combine other pieces, and probably this fragment is from yesterday and another might be from a year before. There are many ways of writing music."

Sakamoto, one of the most famous Japanese internationally, is scathing when it comes to Japan's efforts to promote its culture overseas.

"When Japan introduces its culture to world, it's always something like kabuki

最も国際的に知られた日本人ミュージシャン、坂本龍一。78年からYMOのメンバーとして活動し、5年間に11枚のアルバムをリリース。テクノポップというジャンルを確立した。自分現在も様々な活動を続ける「教授」だが、「ミックジャガーのように」60歳になってまでポップをやる気はない」と言い切る。ブライアン・イーノの音楽をポップと呼ぶなら、ほかの60代の音楽はその方向に近いだろうと教授本人は語る。でも今は違う。ほかのアーティストがやるイングがやるまいが僕には関係ないことだけど、曲作りにドラッグはいらない。必要なものではないんだよ」と語る。また、作曲にはコンピューターを使い、浮かんだときに貯めたセグメントを統合して曲を書く。つまり、同じ曲中に昨日思い浮かんだパートもあれば去年作ったパートもあるということだ。

For somebody whose nickname is the professor, Sakamoto is actually a pretty funny guy, with a definite streak of self-deprecation. Just ask him about his acting career:

"I was really shocked when I saw my acting for the first time (in Nagisa Oshima's Merry Christmas, Mr. Lawrence), because my acting was bad. Maybe I'm the most critical person in the world about my acting. So I decided not to act anymore. And then Bertolucci asked me to act in The Last Emperor. And I couldn't refuse, because I love

But at this moment, I don't. Artists don't need drugs to create music. It's not necessary. I don't care if some artists take drugs. That's their business."

Sakamoto says electronic music doesn't have to be cold.

"I can put my emotions into keyboard-oriented music. That's not hard. I wrote the soundtrack to the TV series "Wild Palms," which was produced by Oliver Stone. It was a weird story. Scary. And that soundtrack was made all on keyboards. No human artists. But the music was pretty moving, I thought."

or sumo," he notes disdainfully. "I guess for the bureaucracy, [things like that] are safe. But as for things like new music, they're probably afraid of that."

After spending the past several years in New York, Sakamoto is contemplating a move back to Japan.

"I have kids, so I want my kids to learn kanji. I'm thinking of [returning to Japan to live]. I haven't decided....

"But I'm always pissed off wherever I go."

METAL + HARD ROCK

Heavy metal and hard rock aren't in short supply in Japan, although you wouldn't know it to look at the pop-dominated charts. An evening of deafening power-chord rock in the local "live house," or a visit to the guitar stores of Tokyo's Ochanomizu district, where Malmsteen and Slash wannabes can always be found showing off their chops in the practice rooms, offer ample proof of metal's continuing popularity in Japan.

What sets Japanese heavy metal and hard rock apart from that of other countries is its tendency toward gothic theatricality. Bands like X Japan, Kuroyume, and Luna Sea, with their elaborate costumes and heavy make-up, have gone well beyond acts like Kiss in emphasizing cartoon-like imagery as much as if not more than musical content. The result is the bizarre sub-genre called visual rock.

ヘビーメタルとハードロックは異色の存在で、巷のライブハウスや御茶ノ水などの楽器店の練習室で、耳をつんざくような音で演奏している彼等の姿をよく目にする。チャート上ではポップが主流だが、巷ではメタルやハードロックの人気も根強い。他の国との大きな違いは、彼らがゴシックを意識した演出とルックスにこだわっている点だろう。例えばX Japanや黒夢、Luna Seaなどのバンドはかつてのアメリカの人気バンドのKissのように強烈な化粧をほどこし、派手な衣装に身を包む。リアリティーのない漫画のキャラクターといえなくもない彼らの姿。しかしその結果、奇妙にもビジュアルロックという新しいジャンルが誕生した。

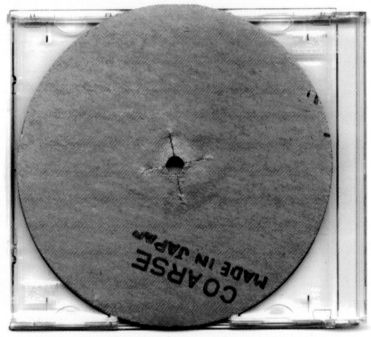

X JAPAN

ビジュアルロックのパイオニア的存在といえば間違いなくX Japanである。彼等の音楽はスピードメタルと表現するのが最も適切だが、同時にメロドラマ風のバンドイメージもうまく調和している。少女マンガから飛び出してきたような女性的なイメージを持つメンバーのYoshikiは、つねに女性ファンの注目の的だ。彼は『Eternal Melody』というクラシックのアルバムもリリースし、多才ぶりを発揮している。

Their music is perhaps best described as speed-metal

The group that more than any other pioneered visual rock in Japan is X Japan (the "Japan" bit was added in order to avoid confusion with L.A. new wave act X during an abortive attempt to market them in the U.S. in the early '90s).

It's hard to say what's weirder—the onstage get-ups of X Japan's members (drummer Yoshiki favors a tres decadent look, complete with pearl necklaces and lace stockings), or the heavy glam-goth look (oversized crucifixes and other tacky jewelry, quasi-bondage gear) affected by the band's mainly female fans.

X Japan's future is uncertain, as individual members like guitarist Hide increasingly concentrate on their successful solo careers. In 1996, the group released its first album in five years, *Dahlia*.

Their music is perhaps best described as speed-metal, and in keeping with the band's image, it's highly melodramatic—a sampling of X Japan song titles should give some idea: "Sadistic Desire," "Endless Rain," "Evening of Despair"...

They're also one of the few Japanese bands to make a point of starting their concerts late, which helps increase a sense of expectation among their fans.

The big news for X Japan aficionados a while back was that Hide, Yoshiki, and lead singer Toshi had cut their hair. Millions wept.

Yoshiki, who is known for collapsing on stage, is the focus of attention within the group. His highly androgynous image—which could be straight out of a girls' *manga* comic book—makes his female fans go completely nutzo. A few years ago he recorded a "classical" album with George Martin (of Beatles fame) and the London Philharmonic Orchestra titled Eternal Melody that highlighted his interest in "serious" music.

The members of Tokyo metal band Piass found out the hard way about the difference between fantasy and reality

The bodies of Piass members Tomohiro Katsui, 28, and Hiroshi Murata, 26, were pulled from Tokyo's Sumida river two and a half hours after they and about eight others jumped 20 meters from a bridge in a video-shooting stunt that went tragically wrong.

Another member of the band, Munehisa Takeda, 24, was reported to be in serious condition following the incident, which occurred after filming began at 1 P.M. Seven other people, including staff members of the local independent record label to which Piass was signed, were able to swim ashore.

Reportedly, all those who jumped into the river were wearing street clothes, and no safety precautions had been taken.

ビジュアルロックグループのもうひとつの成功例はLuna Seaだ。異なる点は、比較的ポップ調であるというところだろう。一方、メタルバンド Piass は現実と幻想の間をさまよったバンドだ。メンバーの内２人が溺死し、他のメンバーも負傷。95年10月25日、ビデオの撮影で東京の隅田川に飛び込んだメンバーに悲劇が待っていた。

Another very successful visual-rock act is Luna Sea (geddit?), whose sound is more poppy than that of X Japan. However, they have the same kind of dark, gothic image, and their songs are full of appropriately mysterious imagery:

Inoue) when they left high school. The current line-up dates from 1989, when guitarist Sugizo (Sasuhiro Sugihara), drummer Shinya (Shinya Yamada, previously with the band Pinocchio), and vocalist Ryuichi (Ryuichi Kawamura,

Held by thousands of stars, always shouting for romance The rusted time floating, you were really shivering.

The band, which was first called Lunacy, was formed in 1986 by bassist J (Jun Onose) and Inoran (Kiyonobu

formerly with Slaughter) joined, paving the way for their major-label debut on MCA Victor in 1991.

HARD-ROCKIN' GALS

Japanese women—delicate and demure, right? Wrong, at least when it comes to the distaff side of the heavy metal/hard rock genre in Japan. Precisely because Japanese women have traditionally been expected to be all sugar and spice, when they reject that stereotype, they tend to do so with a passion—and the music scene is no exception. The late-'80s band boom, for example, produced some truly awesome female rock bands like Show-Ya, Jaco: neco, and the Passengers.

The now-disbanded Jaco: neco (the name meant musk cat) played some of most intense rock 'n' roll imaginable. Guitarist Rosa combined screeching, impassioned vocals and incredibly fast riffing, while genuinely frightening, heavily mascara-ed synth bassist Devil pounded out doom-laden lines that seemed to have come straight from the Grim Reaper Academy of Music, and the very, very inaccurately named Grace smashed the drum kit like a dozen John Bonhams. Jaco: neco released a series of indies albums but never made it into the big leagues, probably because they were just too extreme for any major label.

Just why the Passengers never made it, however, is something of a mystery. Their approach was very traditional in terms of the hard rock idiom. They boasted a great vocalist in Miki Ohno, who despite her diminutive stature belted out Valkyrian vocals on original tunes as well as great cover versions of songs like Jefferson Airplane's "Somebody to Love." Junya Morinaga played inventive, powerful guitar, as opposed to merely bashing out the same old chords. Ohno played guitar too, by the way, providing a further contrast to the stereotypical image of a Japanese female pop star.

In 1993 a four-woman band from Hokkaido called Supersnazz released an album of stripped-down, three-chord rock on famed Seattle indie label Sub Pop. Titled (rather appropriately) *Superstupid!*, it contained gems such as a version of the Rivingtons' no-brain classic "Papa Oom Mow Mow" and Link Wray's "Comanche." Despite various contractual snafus, Supersnazz are still on the scene.

And just when the success of Namie Amuro, et al had made everybody think Okinawa had turned into some sort of idol assembly line, at the end of 1996 along came female vocalist Cocco with a blast of hard, screaming rock from Japan's southernmost prefecture.

Her self-penned lyrics couldn't be less like those voiced by her idol contemporaries:

Her music is dense slabs of grungy guitar over which 19-year-old Cocco (pronounced "ko-ko") wails with a passion that's almost embarrassing. Whether she catches on with the great Japanese public or not remains to be seen.

Another recent entry in the tough-girl category is Osaka native Nanase Aikawa, who's signed to Avex's Cutting Edge label. Her music is a little less out-there than Cocco's, but her persona, especially on stage, is definitely in the don't-fuck-with-me vein. Her debut album, RED, was released in July 1996.

```
I want to put your arms around me,
Tangle around you,
Tear you apart, break you,
seduce you tenderly, damage you,
Strangle you and
Sink your head in  the ocean we saw
together.
```

日本女性は優美で控え目？　少なくともハードロックやヘビメタの世界ではそれは当てはまらない。80年代後半のバンドブームは Show-ya、jaco:neco、Passengers といったすさまじい女性バンドを生みだした。加えて、96年には安室奈美恵や MAX を排出したアイドルの宝庫沖縄から19歳の少女 Cocco がデビュー。北海道からは Supersnazz。加えて、大阪出身の相川七瀬もパワフルな女性ロッカーの一人だ。

SHEENA AND THE ROKKETS

日本女性は優美で控え目？　少なくともハードロックやヘビメタの世界ではそれは当てはまらない。80年代後半のバンドブームは Snow-ya、jaconeco、Passengers といったすさまじい女性バンドを生みだした。96年には安室奈美恵やMAXを排出したアイドルの宝庫沖縄から19歳の少女 Cocco がデビュー。北海道からは Supersnazz。加えて、大阪出身の相川七瀬もパワフルな女性ロッカーの一人だ。

The doyenne of female Japanese rock singers is without a doubt Sheena, of Sheena and the Rokkets. No other Japanese rock singer—male or female—can belt it out quite like this banshee from Kyushu.

The Rokkets' music is pure, no-bullshit rock 'n' roll, at the core of which is Makoto Ayukawa and his trusty Les Paul.

Sheena and the Rokkets were formed way, way back in 1978 by Sheena and guitarist Ayukawa (to whom she is married, by the way). In November of that year, they got a major break by being chosen to back Elvis Costello on his first tour of Japan.

Since then they've remained stalwarts of the Japanese rock scene, playing college festivals, the Budokan, live houses, and, every New Year's Eve, Yuya Uchida's New Year's Rock Festival at a down-at-the-heel theater in Tokyo's Asakusa district. They are, quite simply, The Real Thing and one of the best live rock acts in Japan.

Street
Sliders

Just Rock

the surf
coasters

ハーツ。近年では The Yellow Monkey が直進ロックの代表といえる。しかし、多くが認める最高の硬派バンドは「the little Stones」とも呼ばれたストリート・スライダーズだろう。一方、ファンクメタル系の Gusty Bombs は名前こそひどいが Guns'N Roses ばりのパワフルなバンドだ。

Gusty Bombs

Eschewing glam for musical substance is the unfortunately named funk-metal outfit Gusty Bombs. The Gusties, as they are known by their very loyal fans, made their major-label debut in 1994. Their image used to be very much in the thuggish Guns 'N Roses vein, but these days they've toned things down a bit (i.e. they've cut their hair and bought new clothes), but the music is as powerful as ever. All too often, once Japanese hard rock bands get into the studio, their music loses a lot of its power as the corporate production process takes over and all those annoying rough edges (read: originality and balls) are smoothed out. Not so with the Gusties, fortunately. Now if they'd only do something about the name...

Many Japanese rock bands are confident enough in their music to eschew theatrics and instead just play basic rock 'n' roll. One classic example was now-defunct group the Blue Hearts, who broke up in 1995. Blue Hearts singer Hiroto Komoto and guitarist Masatoshi Mashima have since gone on to form a new band called the High-Lows, which mines the same three-chord rock vein. Another good straight-ahead rock band is the oddly named The Yellow Monkey, who boast an excellent, riffmeister-type guitarist in Hideaki Kikuchi.

The wacky rock sub-genre known as surf music experienced an unexpected renaissance in Japan in 1995 as bands like the Surf Coasters, led by the lightning-fingered Shigeo Naka, introduced another generation of Japanese to classic tunes like "Pipeline" and "Let's Go Trippin'" as well as originals such as "Tsunami Struck."

The band that many consider Japan's best no-frills rock outfit is the Street Sliders, a four-piece group from Fuchu, in western Tokyo, who've been around since 1979. Lead singer Hiroaki Murakoshi has the kind of whiskey-and-tobacco-soaked voice that other rock singers would kill for, while guitarist Kohei Tsuchiya is a brilliant exponent of the Keith Richards riff-after-riff style. No wonder they were given the nickname "the little Stones" when they started out. The Sliders also play very cool reggae when they've got a mind to.

One of Japan's best—if not the best—guitar players is Char, who made his debut while still a teenager and has since gone on to become a respected figure on the Japanese musical scene, mainly through his work with power trio Pink Cloud. Char's best known for his spacey-yet-funky guitar sound—think of Jimi Hendrix and Robin Trower. He also sings in English. Char leads another group, Psychedelix, which comprises drummer Jim Copley and bassist Jaz Lochrie, both from Britain, plus Char.

Char (born in Tokyo in 1955) formed his first band, which covered tunes by the likes of Cream, at the rather precocious age of 11. By the time he was in junior high school, he was working as a session guitarist. In 1974 he formed the legendary band Smokey Medicine with (among others) female vocalist Mari Kaneko and Yoshihiro Naruse.

He released his first solo album, *Navy Blue*, in 1976 and did a Japan tour with Tetsuya Yamauchi, formerly bassist with the Faces. In this era Char's music somehow straddled the divide between hard rock and kayokyoku, which just goes to show how versatile a musician he is. In 1978 he formed seminal band Johnny, Louis and Char (J, L & C) with drummer Johnny Yoshinaga and bassist Louis Kabe. The following year, 14,000 people tried to get into a J, L & C free concert at Tokyo's Hibiya Ya-on amphitheater (normal capacity: about 2,600)—a record for the venue.

Char and
Pink Cloud

THE MAD CAPSULE MARKET'S

4 PLUGS

If thrash metal is your cup of tea, then look no further than the extremely energetic Mad Capsule Market's (the wonky apostrophization seems to be *de rigueur* in Japanese-English). Think Rage Against the Machine, White Zombie, etc., and you'll have a pretty good idea of where these guys are coming from. Their album "4 Plugs" is an awesome demonstration of their powerful-but-tight style. And many of their songs are in English—not that it really matters, since vocalist Kyono attacks a tune in a way that suggests Godzilla clearing his throat.

B'Z and
The Being Sound

In the early '90s, production company Being was the home of a number of major rock acts such as B'z and Wands. Two-man unit B'z (guitarist, Tak Matsumoto, and vocalist Koshi Inaba) was the biggest of these, racking up hit after hit. B'z—with Matsumoto on guitar and Koshi Inaba on vocals—played a rock with a sometimes heavy pop-rock blend that attracted a horde of (overwhelmingly female) fans. B'z's position at the forefront of the once-now ubiquitous production houses, although B'z continued to be an important player on the Japanese music scene.

日本の名ギタリストの一人、Charはジミ・ヘンドリックスやロビン・トロワーのようなスペーシー且つファンキーなギターを弾く。主にPink Cloud での活動で有名。一方、Mad Capsule Market'sはRage Against the Machine や White Zombieを思わせる。アルバム『4 Plugs』は彼らのパワフルで締まった音を聴かせてくれる。90年代初頭にはBzやWands等がプロダクションBeingから生まれ活躍した。

日本の肥沃なクラブシーンは多くのミュージックトレンドを作り出す。テクノやレゲエのようにメジャーでブレイクしたものもあれば、クラブシーンでのみ嗜好されるものもある。いずれにしても、共通して言えるのは在り来りのロックやラップ、アイドルの歌う可愛いだけのポップ・ミュージックとは一味違うということだろう。中でもとりわけ東京のクラブシーンは良い意味でエリート的に流行を作りあげている。そして、その動きの中心となっているのが、各クラブをクールに、そして個性的にするＤＪ達。アシッドジャズは激しい打ち込みのテクノやハウスに対抗して人間的な温もりをピアノやホーン、心地よいジャズファンクのリズムに求めた結果。英国のアシッドジャズレーベル「Talkin Loud」や「Straight No Chaser」等の雑誌はオリジナル・ラヴ、クールスプーン、ユナイテッドフューチャーオーガニゼーションのようなクラブ系サウンドに大きな影響を与えた。

TOKYO'S

CLUB SCENE

The club scene is one of Japan's most fertile sources of new musical trends. Some styles—techno and reggae, for example—break out of clubland into the mainstream, while others remain the preserve of the clubbing cognoscenti. What they all have in common is a sense of subtle sophistication that distances club sounds from both the excess of in-your-face genres like rock and rap and the mindless cutesiness of much mainstream Japanese pop.

The Tokyo club music scene is elitist in the best sense of the word, charting out new territory in advance of the broad mass of music fans. At its heart are the DJs, the people whose ability to pick the right tune at the right time gives a club its identity, the crucial vibe that makes a club cool. One type of club music, acid jazz, started out as a reaction against the heavy electronic beat of techno and house, preferring the warm, resonant tones of pianos and horns, set to a jazz-funk beat that keeps the body moving. U.K. acid jazz labels such as Talkin' Loud and magazines like *Straight No Chaser*, had a major influence on Japanese club acts like Original Love, Cool Spoon, and United Future Organization.

Crucial Japanese acid jazz tracks include UFO's inspired mutation of Van Morrison's "Moondance." Over a finger-snappin' beat and horn parts that sound like they're from a French New Wave film soundtrack, rapper Claudia H. intones a slinky, sultry rap in Portuguese that instantly conjures up images of smoky nightclubs full of people wearing turtlenecks and dark glasses. Acid jazz's spiritual debt to the '50s beatnik scene comes through loud and clear here. Or how about Major Force's "Evil Moon," a spacey, atmospheric track that combines such disparate elements as bird calls, fretless bass, and a Wurlitzer organ played through a Leslie speaker, all set to an infectious, laid-back groove.

UFO's Toshio Matsuura theorizes that acid jazz caught on with young Japanese because they don't care about maintaining strict boundaries between musical genres.

While the "acid" tag comes from the hallucinogens favored by London clubgoers, the drug of choice for most Tokyo clubgoers remains good old alcohol, with maybe the occasional espresso to revive flagging batteries.

"Because Japanese people are interested in categorizing everything, artists called their music 'acid jazz' so the media had a convenient label," says one Tokyo clubgoer.

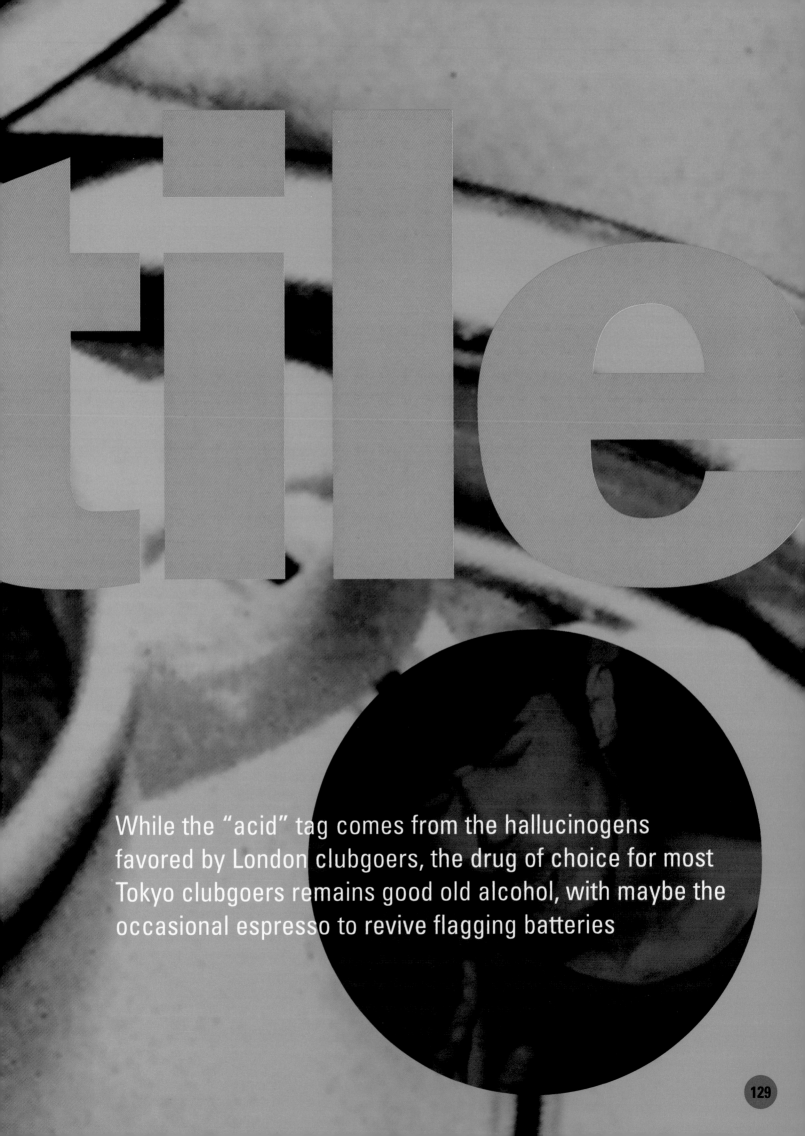

tle

While the "acid" tag comes from the hallucinogens favored by London clubgoers, the drug of choice for most Tokyo clubgoers remains good old alcohol, with maybe the occasional espresso to revive flagging batteries

United Future Organization (UFO) has had the most international impact among Japanese acid jazz acts.

UFO—Tadashi Yabe, Toshio Matsuura, and Raphael Sebbag—have been in the vanguard of the loosely defined acid jazz movement since the early '90s, educating a generation of Tokyo clubgoers in the "rare groove" ambience of classic tracks from the past.

UFO started out as an event/music production company back in the early '80s. In 1991, the trio decided to start making their own records instead of only spinning other artists' platters at Tokyo clubs (which they continue to do at trendoid venues such as Yellow and Blue).

To UFO, what makes the Tokyo club scene so vital is its cosmopolitan nature. "We can get information from other parts of the world quite fast," says Sebbag. Adds Matsuura:

"We are unconscious of our nationality. When we play or record we don't think, 'Oh, this is going to be a hit in this country or that country.' For our generation, 'original' means an original mixture created from old materials. We don't play any musical instruments. For us, a turntable, a record, a sampler or a computer are instruments."

Sebbag thinks Japanese record companies are starting to pay more attention to club music, but Matsuura believes the majors move too slowly to pick up on fast-breaking trends.

"With the big companies you always have to wait for everyone to put their seal on the proposal before you can go ahead with something," he says, hastening to add that he feels a smaller company like Mercury Music Entertainment, to which UFO is signed, is less prone to that sort of inertia.

UFO（矢部直・松浦俊夫・ラファエル・セバーグ）はクラブを中心としたアシッドジャズブームの先駆者として90年代初期より、過去のクラシックをサンプリングしてきた。80年代初期にプロダクションとして結成されたが、やがてアルバムを作るようになる。3人は今でもクラブでDJとして活動を続けている理由の一つは、クラブシーンは国籍やジャンルを問わずに様々な音を融合しオリジナリティを出せるからだと言う。

Best known internationally for having been one-third of Deee-Lite, Towa Tei suggests the quintessential *otaku* nerd, with his outsized black-framed glasses and pageboy haircut. And like any self-respecting otaku, he's fascinated with technology. But Tei's also got an incredible ear for music, which has made him one of Japan's most respected DJs and producers.

Tei's main contribution to Deee-Lite (where he was known as "Jungle DJ Towa Towa") was his innovative and inspired use of samples–bits from old records he remixed into a new piece of music.

In 1994 he released his first solo album, *Future Listening*. Tei co-produced a couple of tracks on Minogue and former YMO member Haruomi Hosono. Tei refuses to be categorized as a musician. "I think a lot of people have an image of me as a house artist," he says, " but I like hip-hop as much as I like house. I've been listening to many types of music, especially easy-listening music. I'm into house, hip-hop, reggae, and bossa nova."

Like Quincy Jones, Tei is very much in the background on his solo work, creating different musical settings in which a wide variety of artists expand on his musical vision. It remains to be seen whether he can (or wants to) make the transition from clubland to mass popularity à la Tetsuya Komuro.

Deee-Liteのメンバーとして海外でもその名を知られるテイ・トウワの外見は、大きな黒縁メガネとおかっぱ頭の「おたく」そのもの。しかし、その音楽センスは彼を日本で最も尊敬されるＤＪ・プロデューサーにした。サンプラー、ターンテーブル等を使って見事にハイテンションな音のコラージュを作り上げるライブは人を惹き付ける。クラブシーンを飛びだし第２の小室哲也となるか（もしくは、なりたいと思うか）。これからが注目される。

TOWA TEI

Sakamoto's *Heartbeat* album and in 1993 he remixed tracks from YMO's *Technodon* reunion album, Pizzicato Five's *Bossa Nova 2001* album, and Sandii's 1994 album, *Dream Catcher*. He's also produced Japanese pop-glam outfit SP-1200. "When I first started with Deee-Lite, I didn't think it would take so much of my time. So, I got kind of tired of it, and decided to take a break from the band," Tei was recently quoted as saying. A key element in Tei's talent is his ability to find good people to work with. For example, on his 1997 album, *Sound Museum*, a track called "German Bold Italic" features the unlikely combination of Australian singer Kylie

Nobukazu Takemura & Bellissima! Records

Some of the coolest club music coming out of Japan can be found on bellissima!, the dance/club label of record company Toy's Factory. The label was launched in 1993, as the Tokyo club music scene took off. Its resident genius is DJ/producer Nobukazu Takemura, who leads the ultracool band Spiritual Vibes, besides producing other artists' work.

Takemura's trademark sound is subtle, spare, and always manages to convey a specific mood, whether it's the sort of early-morning calm suggested by Spiritual Vibes' female vocalist Kikuko Nonaka, or the ennui of a track like "Lethe," with its sinuous rhythm and French-language vocals, which was included in the superlative *Japanese New Vibes* anthology.

In 1994 Takemura released his first solo album, *Child's View*, which was recorded in Tokyo, London, and Paris. It's a tour-de-force, the last word in sophisticated, but accessible late-night-vibe club music.

There's a definite retro, analog vibe on *Child's View*, but the music never slips into the kitsch trip so beloved of Pizzicato Five. Jazz, Brazilian, hip-hop, soul, dance, pop—it's all here. *Child's View* is also beautifully produced—very few records sound this good. This album alone should be enough to silence once and for all those ignoroids who say there's no decent music being made in Japan.

Another bellissima! act is "dub duo" Silent Poets (Michiharu Shimoda and Takahiro Haruno), whose 1995 album *drawing* comprised remixes of their music by overseas luminaries such as Ian Simmonds and Palm Skin Productions as well as Takemura.

Bellissima! products have been released in Europe through Germany's 99 Records, but the label's music hasn't received anything like the degree of overseas recognition it deserves.

Another Toy's Factory label, Idyllic, is home to a well-nigh uncategorizable act called Natural Calamity, whose infectious, laid-back music recalls *Obscured by Clouds*-era Pink Floyd and Primal Scream's *Screamadelica*. This is club music in the chill-out vein, although instead of ambientish synths, Natural Calamity's sound is defined by Kuni Sugimoto's relaxed bass and piano and Shunji Mori's wonderfully understated electric guitar. Sometimes Natural Calamity, who recorded on File Records before moving to Idyllic, rock out in a sort of acidic frenzy, but most of the time they stick to what they call "field music," open-ended sonic meditations that bear repeated listening.

SPIRITUAL VIBES   Natural Calamity

レコード会社トイズファクトリーのダンス／クラブ系レーベル bellissima! は、今最もクールなサウンドを生み出している。93年に始まったこのレーベルでは、主に東京在住 DJ 兼プロデューサー竹村のぶかずはスピリチュアル・バイブという最高にイケているバンドで活動する傍ら、他のアーティストをプロデュースしている。彼のソロアルバム『Child's View』のクォリティの高さは日本の音楽を軽蔑する人々を黙らせるに十分のはずだ。

Charts

In Japan, hit chart data is still largely collected by phone or by fax. Trade paper *Oricon* (short for Original Confidence) plays roughly the same role as *Billboard* in terms of publishing definitive charts. A JVC subsidiary recently signed a licensing deal with SoundScan, the company that collects music-sales data on behalf of *Billboard* in the U.S. to set up SoundScan Japan, which hopes to become this country's first all-inclusive electronic point-of-sale-based (EPOS) chart service. If that happens, people in the Japanese music industry predict the kind of revolutionary impact on the market that the introduction of the SoundScan system had in the U.S.

1 2 3 4 5 6 7 8 9 10 11 12

THE SAIHAN SYSTEM

A key point to note about Japan's international-music market is the difference in price between imports and locally pressed products. CDs manufactured in Japan, whether they are by foreign or domestic artists, are subject to the *saihan* resale price maintenance system. As a result, new CDs by Japanese artists generally sell for between ¥2,800 and ¥3,000, making them among the most expensive CDs in the world. In contrast, imports are not subject to saihan, which means they're usually much cheaper than pressed-in-Japan products.

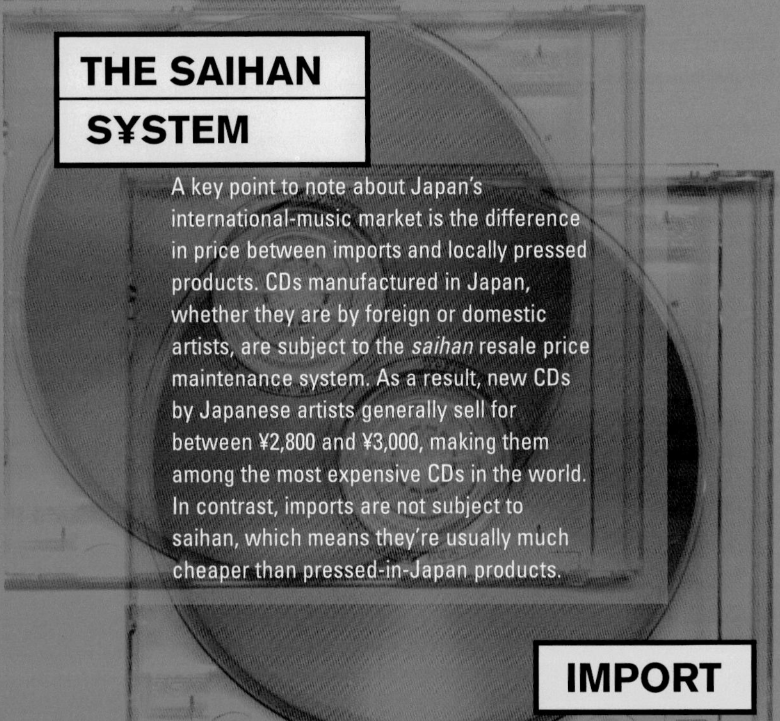

IMPORT

日本のヒットチャートは今だに電話やファクスに頼っている。最近、米国でビルボードの為に総合的なデータ収集とポイント計算を行っているSoundScanが日本に進出。米国同様これが業界に影響を与えることは必至。また、日本の業界について特異な点は再販システムだろう。この再販を免れる輸入盤は千二百円から売られるが、日本人アーティストは勿論、外国人アーティストの国内盤も二千八百〜三千円となってしまう。

JAMMIN' IN JAPAN: THE REGGAE SCENE

日本とジャマイカの共通点といえば、島国であることと頭文字が J なことぐらいだろう。しかし、そんな180度生活環境の違う日本にもレゲエはしっかりと根を張った。ラップと同様レゲエも音楽のみならずファッションのトレンドとして受け入れられている。お馴染みの赤黄緑黒のラスタカラーやマリファナリーフのモチーフは、至るところで目にすることができる（興味深いことに、レゲエという言葉はその固まった長髪がドレッドヘアーに似ているところから、浮浪者を指す場合にも使われている。サンスプラッシュ等の成功によって、日本の音楽ファンの殆どはレゲエを気持ちのいい夏の音楽ととらえており、レコードのセールスはまだまだ限られてはいるものの、ライブはいつも盛況。日本人の若者にとってはレゲエとヒップホップの境目はなく、違うタイプのブラックミュージックとして受け入れられている。

st about all Japan and Jamaica have in common is that they're island countries whose names begin with the letter "J." Everything else—
lture, history, ethnicity—is as different as different can be.

But that hasn't stopped Jamaica's most famous (legal, at least) export—reggae—from putting down firm roots in Japan, whose frenetic style is 180 degrees removed from Jamaica's take-it-easy, level-vibes atmosphere.

Along with rap, reggae is as much a fashion as a musical trend in Japan. The familiar rasta palette of red, yellow, and green set against a black ckground as well as the cannabis leaf can be seen on T-shirts, hats, and posters—wherever Japanese kids hang out.

The word "reggae" itself has even entered the Japanese language, which isn't too surprising, given the Japanese affinity for loan words. Ask a ung Japanese what "reggae" means, and odds are he'll say it refers to one of the homeless men who crowd the underground passageways of in and subway stations—their long, matted hair resembles the dreadlocks favored by reggae artists.

For most Japanese music fans, reggae is simply feel-good, summertime music, as shown by the success of major summer festivals such as ggae Japansplash and Reggae Sunsplash, which feature foreign and Japanese artists.

"There are few people who really love reggae," observes Terumasa Yabushita, an A&R staffer at Ki/oon Sony Records. "Most people treat it as nmertime background music. At clubs and concerts, people don't care who the musicians are. It's reggae, so anybody's OK.

"The Japanese reggae scene is still small, and album sales are low. But the live scene is very healthy."

The fashion aspect of reggae—dreadlocks, the familiar red-green-gold color scheme and the vague hint of rebellion that the music's close ks with marijuana suggest—is probably just as important as the music for many Japanese reggae fans.

Some even go so far as to buy Jamaican-style hats complete with fake dreadlocks attached—just the thing for the rasta salaryman who has to ow up for work at the office on Monday morning.

For many young Japanese, the boundary between hip-hop and reggae is less than clear. Both styles of music are seen as different aspects of ck music.

For others, however, reggae is it. Sadao Osada, for example, has been a fan of the Caribbean music ever since he saw *The Harder They Come* 1978. Osada now mans the turntables on dub nights at Tokyo's Mix club, one of the many small clubs in Tokyo and Osaka that are at the core of e Japanese reggae scene.

"The crowd here at Mix is happiest when I'm playing dancehall-type records," he notes, explaining that reggae rhythms are similar to those of panese festival music, strengthening the connection between the Caribbean musical style and the idea of having a good time.

It was at early '80s clubs like Tokyo's now-defunct Pithecanthropus Erectus that many of the main players in the Japanese reggae scene got eir start. Seminal Tokyo dub band Mute Beat— whose drummer, Yashiki Gota, later joined Simply Red—had come out of the New Wave scene

YASHIKI GOTA

彼の力強い握手と筋肉隆々の腕を見れば、屋敷豪太がドラマーであることは一目瞭然だ。"Groove activator"屋敷は82年に上京して以来Rude Flower、ミュートビートで活動。彼の音楽は様々な要素が組み込まれるが、基本は常にレゲエ／ダブ・マスター。88年には英国にプログラマー・ドラマーとしての活動拠点を移す。以来、Soul II Soulやシンプリー・レッド等と活動、スタジオミュージシャンとして、ソロアーティストとしての活動は周知の通りだ。

You don't have to be a genius to figure out that Yashiki Gota's a drummer. His firm grip and heavily muscled arms are ample evidence of his trade.

The Kyoto native's first encounter with drums was when his father taught him how to play traditional Japanese percussion. In 1982 he moved to Tokyo and joined Rude Flower, which later changed its name to Mute Beat. One of the best heavy dub bands ever, Mute Beat charted new dub territory with its instrumental, horn section-dominated sound, but the band never really achieved anything more than cult status. Gota left the band in 1988 and Mute Beat broke up for good the following year.

Although Gota went on to collaborate with an incredibly wide range of musicians, both in Japan and overseas, his roots are firmly planted in reggae/dub. Not for nothing is he known as the "groove activator."

These days Gota is one of the best known overseas-based Japanese musicians. His foreign connections began when he toured with Japanese band Melon on their European tour in 1983. In 1988 he moved to London permanently and started working as a programmer and drummer with Soul II Soul and Bomb the Bass.

"When I first went over there I felt really comfortable, and was influenced by lots of stuff," Gota recalls. "Because here, there's only Japanese society. But [in] London, there are lots of different types of people and also lots of different musicians from everywhere. I felt really comfortable, although I couldn't speak much English at that time. So when I came back to Tokyo I felt kind of frustrated."

Gota gained wider exposure when in 1991 he became the drummer for pop/soul group Simply Red. In 1993 he released his first album, *Somethin' to Talk About*, which was credited to Gota and the Heart of Gold. Since then he's been incredibly busy as a studio musician as well as spending time on his own music, putting out an incredibly good album in 1995 titled *Live Wired Electro* featuring vocalist Warren Dowd.

To promote that album, Gota put together an unbelievably good band that included the legendary Bernie Worrell on keyboards, and the incendiary Kenji Jammer (another U.K.-based Japanese muso) on guitar. And in 1996, he got back to his dub roots by putting out a great album with Mute Beat trumpeter Kazufumi Kodama titled *Something*.

Like Gota, Tokyo-based band Audio Active have moved beyond their original reggae and dub sound. But Audio Active's sonic journey has taken them into a radically different direction from Gota, as they explore uncharted parts of the ambient and techno soundscapes.

Their first, eponymous album came out in 1993, and was very much in the reggae/dub vein, with tracks like "Free the Marijuana" (a brave gesture in ganja-intolerant Japan) setting a relaxed, spacey mood. The album, which benefited greatly from the patented production style of Adrian Sherwood and Skip McDonald of London's ON-U Sound, included two Hendrix covers: Nona Hendrix's "Space Children" and an ultra-cool version of Jimi H.'s "Burning of the Midnight Lamp." Audio Active continued to work with ON-U Sound on their second album, 1995's *Happy Happer*.

Later the same year they came out with *The Way In Is The Way Out*, a truly weird and wonderful album recorded in collaboration with New Age hammer dulcimer-meister Laraaji. It shows Audio Active at their most spaced-out and adventurous. All too often ambient dub gets stuck in laid-back, nod-out territory, but Audio Active avoid that pitfall by unleashing a steady barrage of richly textured sonic surprises, punctuated by Laraaji's bizarre spoken-word ramblings.

AUDIO ACTIVE

東京ベースの Audio Active も屋敷同様、既成のレゲエやダブの枠には納まりきれない。しかし、それはニューエイジ・テクノの世界という、屋敷の音楽とは全く違う方向で展開されている。93年のデビューアルバムではかなりレゲエ色が濃く、中でも『Free the Marijuana』ではリラックスした心地良い空間を作りだしていた。95年発表の『The Way in Is The Way Out』は彼等の冒険心と浮遊感覚が最も顕著に表われた傑作と言える。

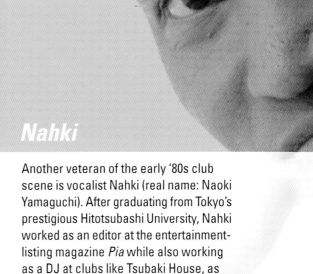

Tokyo Ska Paradise Orchestra

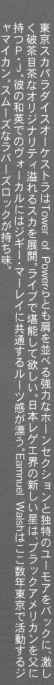

東京スカパラダイスオーケストラはTower of Powerらとも肩を並べる強力なホーンセクションと独特のユーモアをバックに、激しく破茶目茶なオリジナリティ溢れるスカを展開。ライブで堪能して欲しい。日本レゲエ界の新しい星は「ブラックアメリカンを父に持つP.J.彼の和英でのヴォーカルにはジギー・マーレイに共通するルーツ感が漂う。Eamnuel Walshはここ数年東京で活動するジャマイカン。スムーズなラバーズロックが持ち味。

By contrast, the Tokyo Ska Paradise Orchestra (TSPO) favors a harder, more frantic ska sound featuring a strong horn section and a manic sense of humor that makes them true originals and not mere copyists. The 10-member TSPO is best appreciated live. Unlike most Japanese horn sections, which are hopelessly wimpy, they've got what's probably the tightest horn section in the archipelago, ranking right up there with people like Tower of Power. In a sense, they picked up where Mute Beat (MB) left off, opting for a brighter sound than MB's dark dub musings.

Compare, for example, "Dub No. 5," Mute Beat's spacey deconstruction of Dave Brubeck's "Take Five," with TSPO's ska version of the Burt Bacharach/Hal David standard "The Look of Love." On both tracks the musicianship is superb, but you get the sense that the guys in TSPO have their tongues firmly planted in their cheeks, in the same way Pizzicato Five camps it up '60s-style. TSPO is equally at home with rock or soul. And they do a great version of the "Sesame Street" theme song.

One of the most promising artists on the Japanese reggae scene is P.J., whose father is a black American and whose mother is Japanese. This bicultural singer released his first record when he was just 14 and since developed into a strong roots reggae artist whose English- and Japanese-language vocals recall Ziggy Marley.

Among overseas reggae artists active in Japan, probably the most successful is singer Emanuel Walsh, a native of Jamaica who's been a fixture on the Tokyo reggae scene for the past few years. The mellow sounds of lovers' rock are his strongest suit.

On record, he's backed by both Japanese and Jamaican musicians, and the result is a very smooth sound.

Nahki

Another veteran of the early '80s club scene is vocalist Nahki (real name: Naoki Yamaguchi). After graduating from Tokyo's prestigious Hitotsubashi University, Nahki worked as an editor at the entertainment-listing magazine *Pia* while also working as a DJ at clubs like Tsubaki House, as well as recording a single, "Style Echo," with Mute Beat.

Since then he's recorded several impressive albums, which usually sell at least 100,000 copies. Nahki's music is firmly rooted in the fast-rapping dancehall style, and he sings almost exclusively in English, of the heavily accented Jamaican variety—not bad considering he's from the comparative backwater of western Japan's Mie Prefecture.

Nahki often records in Jamaica, where many people assume he's Chinese instead of Japanese, as he describes in his song "Mr. Chin":

"I don't have nothing no againgst no Chinese man.
But Japan a weh mi born and Japan mi come from....
Chinee a Chinee, Japanee a Japanee.
Like how Yardie a no Yankee."

Chieko Beauty

On the ska side of the reggae spectrum is Chieko Beauty, a female singer whose upbeat, melodic style is an interesting fusion of kayokyoku pop and ska.

Like Nahki, Chieko Beauty got her start in Tokyo's revived club scene, specifically at Tools Bar in Tokyo's ultracool Nishi Azabu district in 1991. Unlike Nahki, she sings mainly in Japanese.

"Her music is sweeter, teenager-oriented," says Sony's Yabushita.

80年代初頭からクラブシーンで活躍を続けるNahkiは、三重県出身とは思えないジャマイカンアクセントの英語で歌い、そのスタイルは本格的な速いビートを刻むダンススタイルのレゲエ。印象深いアルバムを発表している。まだまだ草創期であるものの、レゲエはしっかりと日本に根をおろしたのは事実。Audio Activeの大村大助によって作られた『Mambo Presents Yen Town Dreadbeats』は和製レゲエを知るにはうってつけの1枚だろう。

Reggae: Here to Stay

Thanks to the pioneering efforts of musicians like these, reggae is now part of the Japanese musical idiom. For example, female vocalist Sayoko, formerly lead vocalist with pop/rock band Zelda, shifted effortlessly into the reggae vibe with her 1995 album, *Mi Luv Yu*, the highlight of which was a reggae version of the Japanese pop classic "Ue o Muite Aruko" (aka "Sukiyaki"). Backing her were famed reggae artists Sly Dunbar and Robbie Shakespeare.

Other key Japanese reggae acts include the band the Sound Poets, the dance-hall stylist Chappie, and the Tokyo-based band Rankin' Taxi, who a few years back recorded a provocative track "Shinzuru Mono Wa" that called for a "Central Park" to be established in the middle of Tokyo's Chiyoda Ward. That was an unmistakable reference to the Imperial Palace compound, which sits like a green oasis in the middle of the chaotic conurbation that is Tokyo. For Rankin Taxi's sake, it's probably just as well that rightists' musical tastes run more to enka ballads than reggae.

"Shinzuru Mono Wa" was included in a collection of Japanese reggae tracks titled *Mambo Presents Yen Town Dreadbeats* that provides an excellent introduction to Japan's reggae scene. It was put together by Audio Active's Daisuke Omura. Other standout tracks on the album include Mute Beat's "Still Echo (melodica version)" featuring Augustus Pablo on said instrument and Naniwaman's "Jenny," which proves that Japanese-language reggae works.

Meanwhile, publications like *Reggae* magazine contain a wealth of information on all aspects of the music and its historical and cultural background for the serious reggae fan, and clubs such as Hot Co-Rocket, Jamaica, and Kingston in Tokyo as well as others in Osaka keep the reggae flame alive.

RHYTHM
AND
in japan
BLUES

J

APANESE MUSICIANS WHO ARE INTO RHYTHM AND BLUES, SOUL, FUNK, AND THEIR VARIOUS OFFSHOOTS HAVE ALWAYS BEEN IN THE SAME SITUATION AS THEIR WHITE COUNTERPARTS:

M

if you're not black, you've got a credibility problem to overcome. That hasn't prevented a host of Japanese musos from trying their hand at black music through the years, with wildly varying results.

On the negative side, the late, unlamented Bogumbos, specialized in a uniquely appalling travesty of the New Orleans musical tradition, while singer/guitarist Mitsuyoshi Azuma and the Swinging Boppers regularly murdered the jump blues at local festivals.

On the plus side, people like singer/guitarist Fusanosuke Kondo, guitarist Junji Yamagishi, vocalist Mari Kaneko, and harmonica player Weeping Harp Senno achieve a rare degree of subtlety in their music, getting past the surface of R&B and into its emotional core.

日本人のR＆B、ソウル、ファンク系アーティストの悩みは白人と同じ。黒人でなければ本物ではないと思われること。にも関わらず、ブラックミュージックに挑戦する日本人は後を絶たない。もちろん結果は様々。悲惨なところではニューオリンズ・ミュージックに挑戦したボ・ガンボスの解散を惜しむ声はないし、シンガー／ギターリスト吾妻光良やSwinging Boppersは地方イベントの度にブルースの良さを殺してしまった。しかし、シンガー／ギターリスト近藤房ノ介やギタープレイヤー山岸潤史、ヴォーカリスト金子マリ、ハーモニカプレイヤーWeeping Harp妹尾のように、表面的な模倣に終わらず、深い「味」を出すことに成功しているアーティストもいる。

Toshinobu Kubota's ability to transmute black American music into a Japanese idiom HAS MADE HIM ONE OF JAPAN'S BIGGEST STARS.

ブラックミュージックを日本風に変質させる才能が久保田利伸の魅力だ。彼は自分の音楽をヒップホップとファンクの中間、白人のジョージ・マイケルのように、ブラックミュージックに影響を受けたものとしている。現在、久保田はニューヨークに活動の拠点を置く。95年リリースの英語アルバム『Sunshine, Moonlight』はチャートインを果たせなかったものの、『Just the Two of Us』や『Funk It Up』のビデオクリップはアメリカ全土で放映された。

Kubota describes his music as "betwe[en] hip-hop and funk. Some American people tell me that my music is like tha[t] of George Michael—I don't know if that's good or not, but it's a good example for me. George Michael is no[t] black, but he likes black music a lot, a[nd] the result is that his music is pop, but with a black flavor."

That kind of approach has served Kubota well since his mid-'80s debut (which followed an apprenticeship as songwriter). His first album, *Shake It Paradise*, sold more than a million copies in Japan, a feat he repeated w[ith] his next three albums.

In fall 1995, after living in New Yor[k] for two years, Kubota released an English-language album titled *Sunshi[ne,] Moonlight*. A typically polished examp[le] of funk à la Kubota, the album was released in September 1995 on Sony's Columbia label in the U.S. and by Sony Records in Japan. While Kubota was responsible for writing the tunes on th[e] album, he needed help on the lyrics. "[I] still don't understand American people['s] thoughts, because I'm Japanese," he notes, adding, "I like the environment [of] New York—this city has the great vibe[s] I'm looking for."

Although *Sunshine, Moonlight* did[n't] chart in the U.S., videos of album track[s] "Just the Two of Us" (with Caron Wheeler) and "Funk It Up" got some stateside airplay.

TOSHINOBUKUBOTA

QUEEN OF NU R&B
HARUMI TSUYUZAKI

Earthy passion and gutsy delivery are not qualities usually associated with Japanese female vocalists. Cuteness, not technical skill, is what counts. Every so often, though, there comes along a chanteuse who trashes that stereotype.

Harumi Tsuyuzaki, for example. Billed as the "Queen of Nu R&B" in late 1995 (at age 21), she made a stunning debut on the Tokuma Japan Communications label with simultaneous releases of English- and Japanese-language versions of a four-song CD titled *Time*. Commending Japanese singers on their English delivery tends to sound patronizing, but Tsuyuzaki's English vocals are amazingly self-assured and natural-sounding—unlike the efforts of many other Japanese artists. Sure, there are still a few rough edges, but the point is that they are so minor as not to detract from the strength of the overall performance.

Time and Tsuyuzaki's eponymous debut album were recorded in Los Angeles and Tokyo with American and Japanese musicians. Besides being a powerful singer, whether on uptempo numbers or ballads, Tsuyuzaki plays the piano, drums, and sax and also writes and arranges (she co-wrote title track "Time").

While still in high school, she applied to study with famed vocal coach Yuka Kamebuchi, who taught the likes of Toshinobu Kubota, Anri, and Gao. Kamebuchi reportedly said: "There's nothing I can teach you. You may sing as you like."

Tsuyuzaki is very much in the Whitney Houston/Mariah Carey vein, and the music is slickly produced, with that L.A./New York studio polish. Her second album, *Wonder of Dream*, was recorded in New York with local session players, and Tsuyuzaki had a hand in writing most of the music on the album (as well as co-writing some of the lyrics). The entire album is in English, which is a pretty brave gesture, considering that *Wonder of Dream* is, after all, aimed at the Japanese market. Tsuyuzaki is undoubtedly the brightest hope for Japanese R&B in the second half of the '90s.

一般的に日本の女性ヴォーカリストは、テクニックではなく可愛さが大事にされているが、時々この露崎春女のように情熱的でパワフルなシンガーが登場し、ステレオタイプを打ち壊してくれる。95年にニューR&Bの女王と呼ばれデビューした彼女は和英バージョン４曲入りの『Time』というアルバムをリリース。彼女の歌はホイットニー・ヒューストンやマライア・キャリーの流れを受けており、自身で作詞・作曲を手がける。90年代後半の日本R&Bの希望の光である。

彼の場合はジミ・ヘンドリックスやクリームに影響を受けたゴールデンカップスで横浜を拠点に活動。以来、流行に左右されることなくひたすら自分とファンがこよなく愛するロック・ソウルを貫いてきた。恋に破れた男の切なさををを語る名曲「雨に泣いてる」を熱唱する柳にこそ日本のブルースを見ることができる。

GEORGE YANAGI

Singer/guitarist George Yanagi, like many veteran Japanese musicians, started his career during the late-'60s "group sounds" movement, in his case with Yokohama-based band the Golden Cups, who played in the Hendrix/Cream vein. In 1975 he formed the band Rainy Wood, and in 1981 he went solo.

Through the years, he's remained true to the rock/soul style that he and his fans love, ignoring prevailing trends.

In the mid-'90s, his concerts inevitably have an aura of nostalgia, especially since most of his audience are pushing or past 40. He gets a big hand when he says he's going to play songs from 20 years ago.

Yanagi's signature tune is "Ame ni Naiteru" ("Weeping in the Rain"). It describes a heartbroken man whose face drowned in tears as he lingers in the rain. Yanagi pours all his emotion into "Ame ni Naiteru," singing it in his melancholy Yanagi-bushi style, which suits his recurring theme of doomed, fleeting love. This is the real blues, Japanese-style.

YUKADAN

Blues and booze are never far apart, but for Osaka-based band Yukadan, they're inseparable. Singer Atsuki Kimura almost always slings back a few on stage, and his delivery gets more, well, relaxed, as the show progresses, and Kimura croons his way through tunes like "Tokyo Yopparai Blues" ("Tokyo Drunken Blues").

Besides Kimura's mellow way with a tune, the other trademark element of Yukadan's sound is the masterful, understated acoustic guitar of Kantaro Uchida. This four-man band always plays sitting down, although the other three members manage to stay sober. It's the perfect music to enjoy while sitting outside on a hot summer day, drink in hand.

AT FIRST LISTEN THERE IS NOTHING OVERTLY BLUESY ABOUT REICHI NAKAIDO'S MUSIC

REICHI NAKAIDO

He doesn't cover R&B or blues standards, and his own songs aren't usually in the 12-bar style.

But at the heart of his very personal and subtly powerful music is the same kind of bittersweet regret that makes the blues special.

Nakaido first made a name for himself with legendary '70s band RC Succession and in the '80s charted his own very individual musical path with idiosyncratic albums like *The Reichi Nakaido Book*.

His rare live shows have been known to last for as long as four hours, as guests like Kiyoshiro Imawano and Kohei Tsuchiya join Nakaido on stage in what is basically an extended jam session.

Nakaido gives full vent to his love of R&B in his passionately delivered song, "Konya no R&B" ("Tonight's R&B"), whose lyrics mostly comprise a list of his American R&B heroes. It's an amazing track that gradually builds in intensity.

仲井戸麗市の音楽は一見ブルースには聞こえない。R&Bやブルースの名曲をカバーするわけでもなく、彼のオリジナルは12小節パターンでもない。が、そのパーソナルで聴き込むほど味わいのある音楽は、ブルースと同じほろ苦い哀愁に満ちている。ほろ酔いで歌う木村篤のメロウな歌と内田勘太郎の抑えたギターは憂歌団のトレードマーク。ブルースと酒は切っても切れないが、夏の暑い日にドリンクを片手に聴くにはもってこいの音楽だ。

Karaoke is just as, if not more, important than radio as a means of promoting music in Japan. On any given day, six million of Japan's 125 million people can be found crooning their favorite tunes in karaoke bars, hotels, or the industry's latest innovation, karaoke boxes. The singalong craze has grown to where the karaoke industry now has an annual turnover of ¥220 billion.

One clue as to just how crucial a role karaoke plays in the Japanese music biz is the inclusion of vocal-less "karaoke" versions of songs released in the extremely popular CD-single format.

The other one or two tracks are "karaoke" versions of the first two songs, included for the convenience of those who want to practice their vocals before they go off and sing their heart out at a karaoke bar or box.

kara

カラオケ

& Tie-ups

Karaoke has also spread outside Japan, especially in Asia. The word itself has now become part of the English language—"karaoke" is listed in the 10th edition of *Webster's New Collegiate Dictionary*. The biggest karaoke fans used to be middle-aged businessmen singing away their frustrations at the end of a tough day at the office. But in the last few years, karaoke has taken off among younger people and housewives, thanks to the invention of karaoke boxes—small rooms that can be rented by the hour in which groups of friends can have a more intimate singalong experience.

Karaoke, for the benefit of the uninitiated, involves singing with the aid of a mike and an amp to the accompaniment of a prerecorded instrumental track. The word itself comes from *kara* ("empty"), while *oke* (pronounced "okeh") comes from the Japanization of "orchestra"—thus, "empty (i.e. lacking a singer) orchestra."

oke

Taking one's turn at the microphone while drinking with friends or business associates is as much a part of the Japanese way of life as sushi or sumo. But unlike long-established customs such as eating raw fish or watching fat men wrestle, karaoke has only been around since the early 1970s.

The karaoke story begins, logically enough, in a bar.

Back in 1972, a bar ("snack" in Japanese-English) in the western Japanese city of Kobe was in the habit of hiring bands to entertain its customers. However, said bar found that it couldn't afford to pay for an entire band, and so hit upon the idea of using backing tapes for the singers it hired. It wasn't long before customers at such bars wanted to take a turn at the mike — Japanese reserve tends to disappear rather rapidly after the third or fourth *mizuwari* (whiskey and water).

Another reason karaoke caught on is that in Japan there has always been a custom of singing while drinking. So much so, that at first many bar owners were skeptical as to whether their customers would pay money to sing. But the novelty of the medium, as well as later developments such as echo and reverb, made singing karaoke in a bar seem as natural as ordering another mizuwari to most Japanese.

And since so much of the real business of Japan is done in bars, karaoke is a useful way to establish smooth business relations.

今や「karaoke」という言葉はアメリカの有名な辞書ウェブスターにも載っている。70年代初頭に神戸のあるスナックがバンドを雇って始めたカラオケ。時代の変化と共にテープやＣＤ、またＬＤと形を変え進化していった。しかし、いつの時代も酒がカラオケと共にあることだけは変わらない。カラオケビジネスは成長を続け、今や日本では毎日６百万人以上の人が、カラオケを熱唱し、業界の売り上げは年間２２００億円を超えている。88年に岡山県で生まれたカラオケボックスも今日では全国で10万室以上にものぼる。

147

karaoke
Madness

Japanese karaoke culture continues to evolve in interesting and sometimes decidedly odd ways.

Some karaoke fanatics, for example, buy their own personal microphones – sometimes gold-plated – to impress their friends and colleagues with their dedication to the karaoke muse.

You can also buy a special cloth with which to clean your personalized microphone.

There are even karaoke schools where you can improve your vocal skills before going out for a drink with that important client. "The most important thing is how closely you can imitate the song's original vocal," says a spokesman for a karaoke software association. "You can't refuse if your boss or an older person calls on you to sing."

On Valentine's Day a few years back Pioneer introduced a machine that allows customers to record their vocals and the karaoke backing track onto a recordable CD single – the ideal souvenir of a karaoke box singing session.

Karaoke machines can be found in the most unlikely places. Some Japanese McDonald's franchises, for example, have karaoke equipment on hand for children's birthday parties.

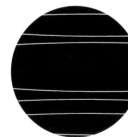

At the other end of the age spectrum, some retirement homes in Japan have found karaoke to be a stimulating activity for elderly people. Technological developments continue to widen the karaoke industry's horizons. More and more karaoke bars and boxes are connected to central databases via ISDN links, eliminating the need to buy large amounts of karaoke software.

Meanwhile, police were recently reported as saying that the karaoke boom has led to fewer arrests for public drunkenness. Seems that folks who've had one or more drinks too many are more apt to spend time working out their stress singing karaoke instead of losing control of themselves in public.

Imagine Mariah Carey chugging down a brewskie in a beer commercial—pretty unlikely, right? But if La Carey were a Japanese pop star, odds are you'd see her hawking everything from soup to nuts on the tube, in magazines and in subway and train advertisements.

In Japan, selling out is no big deal.

In fact, to the Japanese music-biz sensibility there's no such thing as "selling out": endorsing a product or letting your music be used in a commercial "tie-up" is part of the overall promotional strategy for an album or single. One reason tie-ups are so important in the Japanese market is the relative weakness of media like FM radio and MTV. Japan, with 125 million people, has only 47 FM stations, while the U.S., with a population of over 250 million, has more than 7,000 FM outlets. And specialized music TV channels like MTV Japan and Space Shower TV have viewership of under two million households each; get your song used in a TV commercial, on the other hand, and you're pretty well guaranteed a chart position.

It doesn't matter how big the acts—the members of Dreams Come True, one of Japan's biggest groups, regularly praise the virtues of Suntory beer on TV and in print ads.

While the tie-up system can give a song incredibly wide public exposure, it does have its drawbacks. Artists frequently have to give up their performers' royalties in exchange for getting their single used in a commercial. Who pockets the royalties? The music publishers and ad agencies that put the whole deal together.

Another concern is that while a tie-up deal can give sales of a single an enormous boost, it can also focus attention on the song instead of the artist—especially if the performer isn't actually shown in the ad.

Tie-Ups

マライア・キャリーほどの大物アーチストがテレビCMでビールを飲み干す。想像できないことだが、日本の音楽業界では当り前。事実、ドリカムはサントリーとタイアップしている。CMとの「タイアップ」はアルバムやシングルセールスの最も有効なプロモーションなのだ。アメリカに比べ、FMやMTVといった音楽メディアが極端に少ない日本では、TVコマーシャルで曲が流れることが、ランキングチャートでの好位置を保証してくれる。

MAKING IT 海外
OVERSEAS

Japanese pop music is finally beginning to be accepted, at least to some extent, outside its native land. But for the most part, it's not the big names who are becoming popular overseas—it's non-mainstream, left-field acts like Shonen Knife, Pizzicato Five, and United Future Organization.

Jポップがようやく海外で受け入れられるようになってきた。しかし、海外で売れるアーティストの多くは、いわゆる国内でのビッグネームではない。少年ナイフ、ピチカート・ファイブやユナイテッドフューチャーオーガニゼーション、彼らは草の根運動的に海外のファンやレーベルとのつながりを強め、その努力が実を結んだ。しかし、一方でメジャー・レーベルはいまだにプロモーションへの巨額の投資が売り上げを左右すると信じ、アメリカ市場への参入を夢見ている。ところが、アメリカの音楽ファンは宣伝ではなく、音楽そのもので選ぶという傾向が強い。そして、Jポップはどうしても「日本的」または「アジア的」過ぎるのだ。

Their strategy has been to patiently develop grass-roots contacts with fans, labels, and media in other countries, while the major labels that handle big-name acts still seem to think that by doling out large amounts of cash for promotion they can make inroads in tough markets like the U.S. Trouble is, music fans have a distressing tendency to ignore hype and decide on their own whether they like a given piece of music. And, with some exceptions, mainstream Japanese pop is just too culture-specific to sell in other countries, especially outside Asia.

Not culture-specific in the sense of being "too Japanese" or "too Asian," but in the sense that the Japanese music industry's tendency to emphasize form (read "cuteness") over content (read "musical skill/originality") makes its product a hard sell in the rest of the world.

The industry, however, usually cites the language barrier as the reason Japanese music isn't more popular overseas. That's ironic, considering that foreign music accounts for roughly 30% of prerecorded music sales in Japan. It is true, however, that the biggest music market of them all, the good old U.S. of A., is remarkably impervious to songs recorded in languages other than English (with the exception of niche markets such as Latin music).

The only Japanese song to have made it to No. 1 on Billboard's singles chart (back in 1963), the late Kyu Sakamoto's "Ue o Muite Aruko," did so by being renamed with the easy-to-remember (and totally irrelevant) title "Sukiyaki" for the benefit of Americans.

Another reason Japanese music hasn't had more of an impact overseas is that the industry really hasn't felt much of a need to promote its product beyond Japan's shores. It's like the American auto industry (before Japanese and European imports really shook things up): with such a huge domestic market, why worry about exports?

The Japanese music market is very fast-paced (a single's lifespan used to be about three months—now it can enter and leave the charts in less than a month), so time spent trying to promote an act overseas is time lost in the all-important domestic market.

Nonetheless, the Japanese majors announce with depressing regularity that they're going to break this or that artist in the U.S. Poor Seiko Matsuda has been through this process twice, both times to no avail. Meanwhile the indies follow a low-intensity guerrilla strategy that more often than not leaves the biggies way behind.

Other Japanese acts, most notably Chage and Aska in 1996's *One Voice* project, have tried to introduce their music to Europe and North America by having artists from those parts of the world cover their tunes in English. It's still too early to tell whether that tactic will work or not.

LEAVING JAPAN

日本を脱出し海外に定住するアーチストが増えている。例えばニューヨーク。アフリカンドラムとジャズサックスに乗せてサルサ調のパンクロックが聞こえてくる。オルケスタ・デラ・ルスは日本のグループでは珍しく、スペイン語で歌う。彼らのシズリングサルサは国内だけでなく本場でのファンも驚くほど多い。多種多様なサウンドやミュージシャンとの出会いがその魅力らしい。93年、国際交流への貢献で国連平和賞を受賞した。

Some Japanese musicians give up on their home country altogether and move overseas permanently. Drummer/producer Yashiki Gota, for example, says he finds it stimulating to live and work in London because there's a wider variety of musicians with whom he can work.

Similarly, the music of rap/minimalist duo Cibo Matto has obviously benefited from the fact that Miho Hatori and Yuka Honda live on New York's Lower East Side, where, as their publicity material points out, "you'll hear punk rock colliding with salsa tripping over hip-hop on top of African drums and avant-garde jazz saxophone."

Other Japanese musicians want to escape what they consider Japan's rat-race atmosphere.

That's one reason New Age keyboardist Kitaro, for example, lives in Boulder, Colorado.

"It's a really nice college town," he says, explaining that he prefers its relaxed vibe to the hustle and bustle of Tokyo or other big cities. And Kitaro thinks it's important to stay in close touch with the American market, since his music sells better in the U.S. than back home in Japan. "I live there—I'm not a visitor," Kitaro emphasizes. "I talk to many artists, producers, and directors who come from Japan to visit the U.S., but they still have the visitor's mentality."

R&B singer Toshinobu Kubota lived in New York for two years before recording and releasing his first English-language album, *Sunshine, Moonlight*, in 1995.

"I wanted to wait to come to America until I thought I could do it properly," Kubota explains. "I wanted to learn English well enough [so] that I could write songs that wouldn't seem like they're just translated from Japanese. Sometimes they are, since I think in Japanese, but I wanted to make an album in a way that people would think of me as a singer first."

Orquestra De La Luz

While it's not unusual for Japanese groups to try their hand at English lyrics, Spanish is something else again. And for a Japanese group to play salsa ... well. But Japan's Orquestra de la Luz, which broke up in 1996, achieved the seemingly impossible, recording sizzling salsa that has proved amazingly popular with Latin music fans both overseas and back home in Japan, with foreign sales in the hundreds of thousands of units.

Orquestra de la Luz were a bunch of Japanese salsa maniacs who started playing Tokyo clubs in the mid-'80s. In 1988 they went to New York to play some dates and found that "la salsa del Japón" was a hit. Fronting the 11-member band was female vocalist Nora, who wrote the songs' Spanish lyrics. Orquestra de la Luz, you'd swear, were from San Juan and not Tokyo. Sometimes the band drew attention to its Japanese-ness, as in its Spanish-language version of Southern All Stars song "I Am a Piano." Orquestra de la Luz toured the Latin world extensively, and in 1993 was awarded a United Nations Peace Medal for promoting international understanding.

THE ASIA CONNECTION

多国籍レコード会社の急速な増加に伴い、日本のポップ界はアジアに目を向け始めた。

近年、東アジアでのJポップ人気は上昇一方。96年、台湾でのドリカムのアルバム『Love Unlimited』の売り上げは二十万枚を越えた。一方、アメリカで活躍する少年ナイフ。カート・コバーンが91年に彼らをツアーに同行させたことがきっかけとなり、一躍マスコミにも注目された。今日では、海外での成功者の先駆者的な存在となった。

As the multinational record companies expand swiftly into Asia, more Japanese labels are realizing it's time to stop dreaming about making it big in America and instead get in on the action in their own backyard.

People all over East Asia have developed a strong liking for Japanese pop music in the last few years, through karaoke, cover versions, CD sales, and concerts.

Some Japanese record labels, such as Pony Canyon and Avex, have been aggressive in setting up Asian networks, while production companies including HoriPro and Amuse have been searching for new talent with pan-Asian potential. In 1992 Amuse organized shows by the Southern All Stars and Bakufu Slump in Beijing—the first concerts ever performed by Japanese rock bands in China.

In 1996, Dreams Come True broke big in Taiwan with its album *Love Unlimited*, which sold more than 200,000 copies there. Until recently, that would have been impossible, as Japanese music, movies, radio, and television were heavily censored or banned in Taiwan, which was a Japanese colony from 1895 to 1945. Such restrictions still exist in Korea, where Japan brutally suppressed local culture during the 1910 to 1945 colonial period.

Shonen Knife and the Indies Route

Shonen Knife were in the vanguard of the current crop of Japanese artists whose music sells overseas, and remain one of Japan's most successful musical exports. In the early part of the band's career the American indies community picked up on their music before anybody in Japan outside of the band's hometown of Osaka had heard of them.

Kurt Cobain invited the band to tour with Nirvana in 1991. L.A. punk band Redd Kross wrote a song called "Shonen Knife" (the girls returned the favor by writing a song called ... "Redd Kross"). The overseas media picked up on Shonen Knife in a big way, but the tone of much of the press coverage was patronizing, in the "so-bad-they're-good" vein, with an unsettling racist/sexist undertone.

As one female Japanese musician noted: "Japanese women overseas somehow become interesting for the most unusual reasons. Actually before (Shonen Knife) there was another silly girl group, Frank Chickens. I think that says more about how it is outside Japan than it does about Japan."

Now that various other Japanese artists have enjoyed some measure of success outside of Japan, Shonen Knife no longer occupy the unique position they enjoyed when they were discovered by American music fans. Being Japanese and a little bit off the wall is no longer enough.

Whether you like the band or not, Shonen Knife showed that by hooking up with the right people and knowing which segment of the market to target, it's possible for Japanese music to gain a foothold in overseas markets.

In the case of Pizzicato Five, for example, New York-based promotion company Medius Entertainment (now known as Chibari Inc.) was instrumental in spreading the word about the duo to such key media as college radio, eventually landing P5 a contract with Matador Records.

Keeping Tabs On Japanese Music

Staying on top of the latest trends in Japanese pop and sorting through the crap to find the good stuff isn't easy, especially if you don't live in Japan or aren't au fait with the Japanese language. **One big problem is the huge number of new releases every month.** Not that I'm complaining, since that means a wide variety of music— good, bad and indifferent—gets released. Just take a look at the office of any Japanese music critic, which will inevitably be crammed floor to ceiling with CDs, most of them probably unopened, and you'll get an idea of what the dedicated fan of Japanese pop music is up against.

Here, then, are a few suggestions as to how you can keep track of this ever-changing, unpredictable maelstrom of music.

stores

If you live in Japan, simply making the rounds of record stores (I prefer the old-fashioned term to the newer "music store," since regardless of the software format, we're still talking about recorded music), especially in a district like Tokyo's Shibuya. It's probably one of the best places in the world to buy music.

Key Shibuya record stores include:

- Tower's main store on Koen-dori (Tower also has stores in Shinjuku, Ikebukuro, Kichijoji, and in other cities all over Japan). Check out the J-pop section on the second floor, which has an excellent selection of Japanese indies.

- HMV's store on Center-gai-dori (other HMV locations in Tokyo include Ginza, Harajuku, Shinjuku, Ueno, and Ikebukuro, in addition to outlets elsewhere in Japan). Likewise, an excellent J-pop section. A good place to keep track of Shibuya-kei artists.

- Reco Fan (branches in Akihabara, Harajuku, Shinjuku, Takadanobaba, Ikebukuro, Shimokitazawa, Sangenjaya, and Kichijoji). On the fourth floor of the Beam building (with two other locations in Shibuya as well). One of the very, very few places where they sell Japanese pop for less than the list price.

- Disk Union (also has stores in Ochanomizu—five branches, Jimbocho, Shinjuku, Shimokitazawa, and Kichijoji). There are two branches in Shibuya. One has a good selection of heavy metal and lots of used CDs.

- Cisco. A great chain that has individual stores specializing in techno, house, imports, etc.

These are just a few of the standout stores in Shibuya. Walk around and discover the many small, specialized record stores there for yourself. One, for example, is very unusual in that it sells Japanese pop albums imported from Southeast Asia, which makes them cheaper than regular domestic releases.

In Tokyo's tony Ginza district, the record store to check out is Yamano Gakki, just around the corner from the Wako building. Good selection of J-pop and (gasp!) a knowledgeable staff.

Up in Shinjuku, go to the west exit of the station and walk down to the seven-chome district, where you'll find a myriad of small record stores, some in apartments, that sell (among other things) Japanese indies and other specialized domestic products.

The big chains, like Tower, HMV, Virgin, Shinseido, and Yamano, all publish their own free magazines highlighting the latest domestic (and foreign) releases. Tower's *Bounce* magazine is particularly informative. Of course, it helps if you can read Japanese, but if you're interested in Japanese music, these magazines are great learning aids.

The key point here is that by browsing through the J-pop sections of these and other record stores, you'll pick up a lot of information—such as what a given artist actually sounds like, thanks to the listening posts at many of the stores.

And if you're Internet-capable, a handy resource is the Tokyo record stores site at: http://www.twics.com/~robbs/rekodoya.html. It's all in English.

Because of the relative lack of FM stations in Japan, radio is aimed at a very wide audience and consequently the music tends to be very mainstream. Don't expect to hear Violent Onsen Geisha on a Japanese FM station anytime soon. (AM radio is talk-oriented for the most part, as anyone who's ever been in a Japanese taxi can attest.)

Nonetheless, listening to FM stations such as J-WAVE, Bay FM, and Tokyo FM will give you a good sense of what most people are listening to.

Radio and

It's the same story with TV—the big networks have to appeal to a wide demographic, and so even middle-of-the-road music programs (the long-defunct "Yoru no Hit Studio Delux" comes to mind) can't compete against the puerile lowest-common-denominator "variety" dreck that dominates prime time. Late-night TV offers more scope for music programs, such as Sony's techno music show.

Cable and satellite TV have yet to take off in a big way in Japan, and as a result MTV and other music-oriented programming have much less of an impact than in other countries. But if you can afford a tuner or live in an area with cable TV service, MTV Japan and Space Shower TV (especially the latter) broadcast lots of Japanese music videos and interviews with domestic artists, as well as provide other useful information about the Japanese music scene.

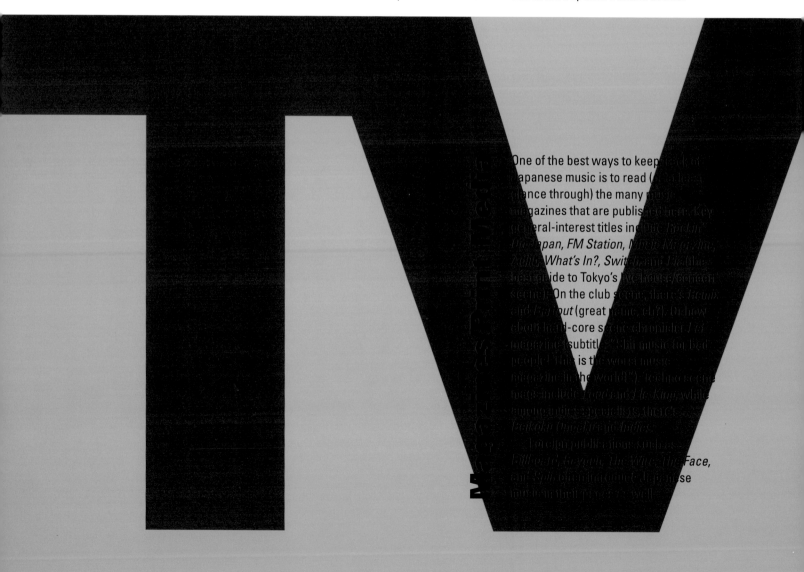

One of the best ways to keep track of Japanese music is to read (or at least glance through) the many music magazines that are published here; key general-interest titles include *Rockin' On Japan*, *FM Station*, *Music Magazine*, *Xcllo*, *What's In?*, *Switch*, and *Pia* (the best guide to Tokyo's live house/concert scene). On the club scene, there's *Remix* and *Far out* (great name, eh?). Or how about hard-core scene chronicler *Fat* magazine (subtitled "Shit music for bad people! This is the worst music magazine in the world!"). Techno scene mags include *Loud* and *Tekking*, while among indies specialists, there's *Beikoku Ongaku* and *Indies*.

Foreign publications such as *Billboard*, *Kerrang*, *The Wire*, *The Face*, and *i-D* often find their way into Japanese fans' collections as well.

The Internet

The Web has become one of the best—if not *the* best—places to keep tabs on new music coming out of Japan.

The amount of information on the Internet about Japanese pop music is truly amazing. English- and Japanese-language Web sites devoted to Japanese music range from pages listing gigs and releases of underground bands such as Violent Onsen Geisha, the Boredoms, and Gore Beyond Necropsy to those put together by fans of idol acts such as Yuki Uchida and Chisato Moritaka.

The Web has become one of the best—if not the best—places to keep tabs on new music coming out of Japan.

One of the best Japanese-music sites is UNSOUND, which owes its existence to ad agency employee Gil Kay. Daytime, he works on a project to develop interactive online ads. At night and on weekends he hangs out in Japan's fervid underground music scene as he seeks new stuff to add to the UNSOUND site.

Kay sees UNSOUND (http://www. atom. co.jp/UNSOUND/) as a logical extension of his efforts in the mid-'80s as a UCLA college radio DJ to introduce the rest of the world to Japanese music.

"In the U.S., Japanese artists weren't too popular yet—the Japanese were seen as businesslike, non-creative people," says Kay, who was born in Los Angeles to Japanese parents and grew up in the U.S. "I'd been exposed to a lot of Japanese creative artists—YMO, RC Succession, etc.—and I just wanted to prove the consensus wrong."

After attending UCLA for two and a half years, Kay enrolled in Tokyo's Hitotsubashi University in 1990 and worked as a DJ at Tokyo FM, playing alternative Japanese music after "forcing" the station's program directors to do so.

"Japanese don't look toward their own artists—they look toward the West," he complains. "I realized that I needed to expose Japanese talent to the Japanese as well."

But after a while Kay realized he'd have to find a medium other than FM radio if he wanted to spread the word about Japanese music beyond Japan.

"Now, with the Internet, I finally have the perfect medium," he enthuses, pointing out that it transcends geographical and linguistic barriers.

UNSOUND got high marks from counterculture guru and Web fan Timothy Leary when Kay met the good doctor in California through a mutual friend some time before Leary's death.

"Gil Kay has just screened for me his magnificent web page, 'UNSOUND,'" Leary wrote in an introduction to the site. "It allows the user to construct and deconstruct sounds and images. This is a breakthrough I have been hoping for… This is the future."

Leary was referring to a feature allowing cybernauts to view works by artists in the site's "SOUND" (audio) and "UNSOUND" (visual) sections, and request the artists if you like what you hear or see. Kay then takes the top three artists from each section and compile them into Quicktime movies—the "Sound" artists become the soundtracks, and the "UNSOUND" artists go into the video tracks.

When UNSOUND made its Web debut in October 1994 it was one of the first Japanese independent-music sites, along with sites such as the Japanese Independent Music Archives (http://www.atom.co.jp/INDIES/), which like UNSOUND has English and Japanese versions.

But as any dedicated Net-surfer knows, the big problem with music-related sites is the amount of time it takes to download sound files—unless you have an ISDN connection. With UNSOUND, for example, it can take about 6 minutes using a 14,400-bps modem to download a 30-second sample of music. Also, you'll need Netscape Navigator 1.1 (or a later version) to get into sites like UNSOUND (Netscape can be downloaded from the introductory portion of the site itself).

Banzai Bonsai!

The best place to start your Web trek into the world of Japanese pop is undoubtedly Bonsai (http://www.hatch.co.jp/di/bonsai/index.htm), which has lots of links to Japanese pop-culture sites. It's particularly strong on idol sites.

And if this book has at all whetted your appetite for information about Japanese pop, check out the Japanese Popular Culture Page's J-pop FAQ site (http://stripe.colorado.edu/~jheath/jpop.html), a collaborative effort by some truly dedicated J-pop fans—amazing!

Most Japanese record companies now have their own Web sites. Sony has one of the better ones (**http://www.sme.co.jp/index.html**), which has a fair amount of English material. Also worth checking out is the high-tech home page for dance label Avex (**http://www.avexnet.or.jp/**). Links to major labels' sites and lots of other information can be found at the rather spiffy Web site of the Recording Industry Association of Japan (**http://www.japan-music.or.jp/**).

The Famous Japanese site (**http://cc2000.kyoto-su.ac.jp/information/famous/**) has biographies of many J-pop stars. And for the latest chart info, check out *Oricon* magazine's site (**http://www.999.com/Oricon/index.html**).

Superproducer Tetsuya Komuro has a very impressive site (**http://www.komuro.net/**) that's full of information about the "Komuro family" of performers.

A good example of a Japanese-music Web site put together by dedicated overseas fans is Shrine to Shonen Knife (**http://www.netropolis.net/shonen/knife/shrine.htm**). It includes color pix, albums, and discographies of Osaka's best female power-punk trio and links to other Shonen Knife sites, which have imaginative names like John's Shonen Knife Page. Or check out New York resident Nicholas D. Kent's excellent Japanese Synthesizer Music page (**http://idfx.com/artskool/jem/**), a true labor of love by someone who obviously knows his subject frighteningly well.

An example of a state-of-the-art fan club page is that

dedicated to Pizzicato Five (**http://www.clark.net/pub/fan/pizz.html**). Very nice-looking indeed.

For concert listings, try Internet English-language magazine Tokyo Q (**http://www1.so-net.or.jp/tokyoq/lastweek.html**).

For the club scene, log on to Tokyo Night Clubbing (**http://www.st.rim.or.jp/%7Eliliko/club.html**) or CyberJapan's Club Info Page (**http://www.bekkoame.or.jp/~tokopi/linkschacha/linksqueen.html**), as well as the Tokyo Club Guides and Music Links site (**http://www.twics.com/~robbs/othclub.html**).

The J-underground site (**http://www.cs.is.sagau.ac.jp/laboratory/kusano/irman/bands.html**), besides containing lots of information about the indies/underground scene, also has a Marketplace section that lets you buy those hard-to-find releases directly from the folks who put the site together. Another great site where you can buy underground Japanese music is Cerberus Japan (**http://www.cdj.co.jp/**).

There's no shortage of information about Japanese pop on the Web—so happy surfing!

Other sites include:

Japanese Musicians, JPOP links (**http://anansi.panix.com/userdirs/tn/j-music2.html**)

Japanese Independent Music Archives (**http://www.atom.co.jp/INDIES/**)

Sheena & the Rokkets' Official Web Site a.k.a. RokketWEB (**http://www.rokkets.com/index.html**). You won't believe the work that Rokkets' guitarist Makoto Ayukawa has put into this site. Incredible links to everywhere in the known (and unknown) musical universe.

Japan Edge (**http://www.ces.kyutech.ac.jp/student/JapanEdge/e-index.html**). Mainly techno.

The Trattoria Sound (**http://neoteny.eccosys.com/PEOPLE/trattoria/entrance.html**). Home page of the Trattoria label, home of Shibuya scene acts such as Cornelius.

And to see what "virtual idol" Kyoko Date is up to, have a look in at her site, which has any number of bells and whistles to keep Net serfs amused (**http://www.damoon.net/star7.htm**).

These sites' addresses could change at any time, of course, so it's best to check them from time to time to see whether they've moved.

While every effort has been made to contact the rights holders for permission to use material that appears in this book, the author and the publisher wish to apologize if they have inadvertently omitted, or failed to approach, anyone.

Photo Credits

7: (the Spiders) Mercury Music Entertainment; (Pink Lady) Victor Entertainment; (Ho.Ja.Ne CD single cover) Sony Music Entertainment, Japan; (Ryuichi Sakamoto) Kab K.K.; (dip in the pool) East Works Entertainment inc.; (Kome Kome Club) Sony Music Entertainment, Japan; (Southern All Stars) Victor Entertainment; (the Eccentric Opera) Sony Music Entertainment, Japan; (Kitaro) Pony Canyon; (UA) Victor Entertainment; (Shang Shang Typhoon) Sony Music Entertainment, Japan; (Shizuru Ohtaka) King Record; (ONTJ) Photo by Toshi Ota; (Lolita No. 18) Benten label; (Hoppy Kamiyama) God Mountain/Photo by Hiroyuki Taneda; (Towa Tei) Yoshimoto Kogyo

8: (Kazuyoshi Saito) Shinko Music; (Tomoe Shinohara) Sony Music Entertainment, Japan

10: (Hibari Misora) Hibari Production

11: (Kafu Kafu Dogo Shico) Pony Canyon

12: (The Tigers) Polydor K.K.; (the Jaguars) Mercury Music Entertainment

13: (The Spiders) Mercury Music Entertainment

16-17: (crowd scene) © Andy Beese

18: (Seiko Matsuda) Mercury Music Entertainment

19: (Seiko Matsuda album covers) Mercury Music Entertainment

20: (Pink Lady) Victor Entertainment

21: (Kyoko Date) Photo © HoriPro

23: (schoolgirls) Courtesy of Masumi Ikeda

24: (Tokio) Sony Music Entertainment, Japan

25: (V6) Avex D.D.; (SMAP) Victor Entertainment

26: (Chisato Moritaka) Coolie Production

27: (Princess Princess) Shinko Music

28: (Yutaka Ozaki) Sony Music Entertainment

33: (UA) Victor Entertainment

34: (Miwa Yoshida) Time Inc. Asia

35: (Dreams Come True) Sony Music Entertainment, Japan

36: (Akiko Yano) Sony Music Entertainment, Japan; (Tatsuro Yamashita) Smile Co.

37: (Great 3) Toshiba-EMI; (Mariya Takeuchi) Smile Co.

38: (Chage and Aska) © Andy Beese; (dip in the pool) East Works Entertainment inc.

39: (Miyuki Nakajima) Yamaha Music Foundation

40: (Southern All Stars) Victor Entertainment

41: (Yumi Matsutoya) Toshiba-EMI

42: (My Little Lover) Toy's Factory

43: (Mr. Children) Toy's Factory; (Spitz) Road and Sky K.K.

44: (Kome Kome Club) Sony Music Entertainment, Japan

45: (UA) Victor Entertainment

46: (The Boom) Sony Music Entertainment, Japan

49: (Shoukichi Kina) Mercury Music Entertainment

50: (Shang Shang Typhoon) Sony Music Entertainment, Japan

51: (Nenes) Antinos Records Inc.

52: (Rinken Band) Sony Music Entertainment, Japan

53: (Soul Flower Union) Sony Music Entertainment, Japan

55: (Shizuru Ohtaka) King Record

57: (Diamantes) Mercury Music Entertainment

58: (Tokyo Bibimbap Club) Toratanu

59: (The Boom) Sony Music Entertainment, Japan

60: (Sandii) Sony Music Entertainment, Japan; (Dream Catcher album cover) Sony Music Entertainment, Japan

61: (Kodo) Sony Music Entertainment , Japan

62-63: (Shibuya street scene) © Andy Beese

64: (Homeless Heart) Sony Music Entertainment, Japan; (Kabocha Shokai) King Records

65: (Kenji Ozawa) Toshiba-EMI; (Kahimi Karie) Polystar

67: (Pizzicato Five) Hougadoh

68: (Cosa Nostra) Toy's Factory

69: (Theatre Brook) Sony Music Entertainment, Japan; (Theatre Brook live pictures) Rie Nakaya

70: (Cornelius) Polystar

72: (Lolita No. 18) Benten label

73: (High Standard)Howling Bull Entertainment, Inc; (Garlic Boys) Howling Bull Entertainment, Inc.; (Petty Booka) Benten label

74: (Hoppy Kamiyama) God Mountain/Photo by Hiroyuki Taneda

75: (ONTJ) Photo by Toshi Ota

76: (Violent Onsen Geisha/QUE SERA, SERA album cover) Toshiba-EMI; (Fully Fed Freaks album cover) Benten label/Illustration by Rockin' Jelly Bean

77: (Benten logo) Benten label

78: (Super Junky Monkey) Sony Music Entertainment, Japan

79: (Super Junky Monkey) Sony Music Entertainment, Japan

81: (Friction) Imagica Media Publishing; (Spoonperm) Michael Wayne Rogers; (Guitar Wolf) ZK Records/Photo by Shigeo Kikuchi

82: (Buffalo Daughter) Buffalo daughter/Minoru Yokoo

87: (trf/Namie Amuro/H Jungle With T) Avex D.D.; (Yuki Uchida) King Record; (Ryoko Shinohara) Sony Music Entertainment, Japan; (Tomomi Kahala) Pioneer LDC

88: (trf) Avex D.D.

89: (Namie Amuro and Max) Avex D.D.

90: (Velfarre) Avex D.D.

91: (globe) Avex D.D.

93: (Scha Dara Parr) Toshiba-EMI

94-95: (Da.Yo.Ne, So.Ya.Na, Da.Ga.Ne, Ho.Ja.Ne, So.Ta.I CD single covers) Sony Music Entertainment, Japan

96: (Vibrastone) I section; (Dassen Trio) Yoshimoto Kogyo

97: (Cibo Matto) People's Records; (m.c.A.T.) Avex D.D.

98: (DJ Honda) Sony Music Entertainment, Japan/Photo ©Hachi

102: (Brand New Knife album cover) MCA Victor Inc.

103: (Shonen Knife) MCA Victor Inc./Photo by V. Berndt

104: (Favorites album cover) MCA Victor Inc.

105: (Nelories) Toshiba-EMI

106: (Shiro Amamiya) Shiro Amamiya/America Mura & Co./Photo by Matthias Ley

107: (Ulfuls) Toshiba-EMI; (Sha Ram Q) BMG Japan Inc.

110: (Ken Ishii) Sony Music Entertainment, Japan/Photo copyright Tatsuya Yusa

111: (Loud cover) XTRA Inc.

112: (Mix-Up Vol.1, Vol.2, Vol.3, Vol.4, and Vol. 5 album covers) Sony Music Entertainment, Japan

113: (Denki Groove) Sony Music Entertainment, Japan

114: (Haruomi Hosono and Miharu Koshi) Mercury Music Entertainment Inc. (Love, Peace, and Trance album cover) Sony Music Entertainment, Japan

116: (Kitaro) Pony Canyon

117: (The Eccentric Opera) Sony Music Entertainment, Japan; (Tomoe Shinohara) Sony Music Entertainment, Japan

118-119: (Ryuichi Sakamoto) Kab K.K.

120: (Nunchaku) Howling Bull Entertainment; (Show-ya) Toshiba-EMI

122: (X Japan) East West Japan

123: (Luna Sea) MCA Victor Inc./Photo by Nicci Keller

124: (Cocco) Victor Entertainment; (Nanase Aikawa) Avex D.D.

125: (Sheena and the Rokkets) Victor Entertainment

126: (Street Sliders/Gusty Bombs) Sony Music Entertainment, Japan; (Surf Coasters) Victor Entertainment

127: (Char) Kui; (4 Plugs album cover) Victor Entertainment

128: (club scene) © Andy Beese

130: (United Future Organization) Mercury Music

Entertainment, (The Planet Plan album cover) Mercury Music Entertainment/Art direction by United Future Organization, design by Icebraker, illustration by Kazuo Hozumi

131: (Towa Tei) Yoshimoto Kogyo

131: (Spiritual Vibes/Natural Calamity) Toy's Factory

136: (Yashiki Gota) Sony Music Entertainment, Japan

137: (Audio Active) Beat Ink

138: (Tokyo Ska Paradise Orchestra/Nahki) Sony Music Entertainment, Japan

139: (Chieko Beauty) People's Records

140: (Harumi Tsuyuzaki) Tokuma Japan Communications/Photo by Kazunari Tajima/Mina Kawagoe

142: (Toshinobu Kubota) Sony Music Entertainment, Japan

143: (Harumi Tsuyuzaki) Tokuma Japan Communications/Photo by Kazunari Tajima/Mina Kawagoe

144: (George Yanagi) MCA Victor/Photo by M. Kawahara; (Yukadan) WEA Japan

145: (Reichi Nakaido) Toshiba-EMI

149: (TV Theme and CM Hit Songs '97 album cover) Sony Music Entertainment, Japan

151: (Shonen Knife) MCA Victor Inc./Photo by V. Berndt; (Pizzicato Five) Hougado; (Seiko Matsuda) Mercury Music Entertainment; (Kitaro) Pony Canyon; (Chage & Aska) © Andy Beese

152: (Orquestra de la Luz) BMG Japan

153: (Let's Knife album cover) MCA Victor

Inside Front Cover: (CD photo) © Amos Wong/Russel Wong Photography

Inside Back Cover: From top left clockwise (Ulfuls) Toshiba-EMI; (Ken Ishii) Sony Music Entertainment, Japan/Photo © Tatsuya Yusa; (Kafu Kafu Dogo Shico) Pony Canyon; (Electro Asyl-Bop album cover) KI/oon Sony Records; (Spitz) Road and Sky K.K.

Song Credits

*Lyrics translated into English by Steve McClure

*28: (Yutaka Ozaki) "High School Rock 'n' Roll"

*30: (Yutaka Ozaki) "Seventeen's Map"

*30: (Yutaka Ozaki) "The Night of 15" Original lyrics in Japanese by Yutaka Ozaki

*53: (Soul Flower Union) "Dance Your Village's Original Dance" Original lyrics in Japanese by Takashi Nakagawa and Hideko Itami

*53: (Soul Flower Union) "Eejanaika" Original lyrics in Japanese by Takashi Nakagawa

78: (Super Junky Monkey) "Spit Bug (Kioku no Netsuzo)"

79: (Super Junky Monkey) "Buckin' the Bolts"

79: (Super Junky Monkey) "Fuck That Noise" Lyrics by Mutsumi Takahashi

79: (Super Junky Monkey) "Get Out" Lyrics by Mutsumi Takahashi and Tim Jensen

*88: (trf) "Love and Peace Forever" Original lyrics in Japanese by Tetsuya Komuro and Takahiro Maeda, © Prime Direction Inc.

97: (Cibo Matto) "Know Your Chicken" Lyrics by Cibo Matto

*97: (m.c.A.T.) "Oh! My Precious" Original lyrics in Japanese by Akio Togashi

101: (Shonen Knife) "My Favorite Town" Lyrics by Naoko Yamano

104: (Shonen Knife) "Twist Barbie" Lyrics by Naoko Yamano

*105: (Nelories) "Neutral Blue" Original lyrics in Japanese by Jun de Nelorie

*123: (Luna Sea) "End of Sorrow" Original lyrics in Japanese by RYUICHI, SUGIZO, INORAN, J, SHINYA

*124: (Cocco) "Kubi" Original lyrics in Japanese by Cocco, © 1996 Stay Gold Music Publishing Inc.

139: (Nahki) "Mr. Chin" Lyrics by Floyd Brown